I am a Mother of three and have three grandchildren with one great grandbaby on the way. Currently I am 81 years young and this is my first published work.

This book is a collection of my favorite homemade and family recipes. Some recipes contain variations to add even more variety to this cookbook. I like to use low sodium based products, natural sea salt and ingredients such as Rumford Baking powd.which contains no aluminum. I prefer organic produce and products when available. I am sure you will enjoy my home style cooking, there is a little something for everyone.

My gratitude goes out to my family for encouraging me and helping me publish this book and being my taste testers through countless trial and error attempts at perfecting these recipes.

Lois M. Dodson-Author

To Owen and June
With Love,
Lois Dodson

TABLE OF CONTENTS

## HUSH PUPPY MINI MUFFINS

¾ cup yellow cornmeal
1 cup unbleached all-purpose flour
1/3 cup sugar
1 Tbsp. Rumford baking powder
½ teaspoon sea salt
½ teaspoon chili powder
1 teaspoon garlic powder
1 cup milk
1 egg beaten
2 Tbsp. canola oil
1/3 cup shredded Monterey Jack Cheese
4 Oscar Myer bun length hot dogs, cut into 1-inch pieces

Preheat oven to 400 degrees F. Coat two 12 cup mini muffin tins with non-stick cooking spray. Stir together the cornmeal, flour, sugar, baking powder, salt, chili powder and garlic powder. Make a well in the center and pour in the milk, egg and oil. Stir until blended, then gently stir in the cheese. Drop a small spoonful of batter into the bottom of each muffin cup. Place a piece of hot dog on top. Fill cups with enough additional batter to cover the hot dog pieces. Bake for 10 to 12 minutes, or until muffins are lightly browned and spring back when gently pressed. Cool slightly before removing from the muffin pans. Serve warm with Fiesta Dipping Sauce.

# FIESTA DIPPING SAUCE

½ cup sour cream
½ cup mayonnaise
1-1/2 Tbsp. taco seasoning mix from a 1.25 ounce package

Whisk together the sour cream, mayonnaise and taco seasoning mix until smooth. Serve immediately with the muffins.

Yield: 12 servings- Per serving (2 muffins)
Note: you can also make these in 1 regular 12 cup cupcake pan. Put 2 pieces of hot dog in each muffin. Bake for 20 minutes. Serve without sauce.

# PIMENTO CHEESE

8 oz. cream cheese softened (1/3 less fat Neufchatel)
1 cup shredded sharp cheddar cheese
1 cup shredded Monterey Jack cheese
½ cup mayonnaise (light)
3 Tbsp. mashed pimentos
2 tablespoons sugar
1 Tbsp. grated sweet onion
¼ teaspoon garlic powder
¼ teaspoon black pepper

With an electric mixer, beat cream cheese until fluffy. Add remaining ingredients and beat until well blended. Place in a glass jar with lid and refrigerate. Serve on crackers or celery. Note: Alternatively, replace 1 cup shredded Parmesan cheese for the Monterey Jack cheese. Yield: Approximately 1 quart

## CHUNKY BLUE CHEESE DIP

1 pkg. (8oz.) cream cheese softened
1/3 cup sour cream
½ teaspoon white pepper
¼ to ½ teaspoon sea salt
1 cup (4oz.) crumbled blue cheese
1/3 cup minced chives or green onions

In a small bowl, beat the cream cheese, sour cream, pepper and salt until smooth. Fold in the blue cheese and chives or green onions. Serve with crackers or apple and pear slices. Yield: 1-3/4 cups

## LIME FRUIT DIP

1 package (8oz.) cream cheese, softened
1 jar marshmallow cream (7oz.)
1 carton (6 oz.) lime custard style yogurt
Assorted fresh fruit

In a small mixing bowl, beat cream cheese until smooth; beat in marshmallow crème. Fold in yogurt. Cover and refrigerate until serving. Yield: 2-1/2 cups

## CHEESE LOG

1-8 oz. pkg. ½ less fat Neufchatel cream cheese
1 cup shredded Parmesan cheese
¼ cup chopped red onion
½ teaspoon garlic powder
¼ teaspoon black pepper
2 Tbsp. fresh parsley

Mix cream cheese, Parmesan cheese, onions, garlic powder and pepper with electric mixer until well blended. Shape into a 6-inch log; wrap tightly in plastic wrap. Refrigerate 30 minutes or until firm. Roll in parsley until evenly coated on all sides. Serve as a spread with Ritz roasted vegetable crackers.

## HAM SALAD

1 cup cooked ham diced into small pieces
1/3 cup miracle whip or light mayonnaise
2 Tbsp. sweet relish
1 Tbsp. chopped sweet onion

Mix all ingredients and chill. Serve on crackers.
Yield: 18 servings
Note: Boiled ham can be substituted. Cut into tiny pieces.

## LIGHT GUACAMOLE

2 large ripe avocados, peeled, divided
1 Tbsp. lemon juice
½ cup fat-free sour cream
¼ cup chopped sweet onion
½ teaspoon seasoned sea salt
¼ tsp. garlic powder

Remove pits from avocados. In a blender, combine 1 avocado, lemon juice, sour cream, onion, seasoned salt and garlic powder and process until smooth. Spoon into a small bowl. Mash remaining avocado with a fork and stir into pureed avocado mixture. Chill. Serve with tortilla chips.

## CUCUMBER SAUCE

½ cup finely chopped, seeded cucumber
¼ cup low-fat plain yogurt
¼ cup finely chopped red or sweet onion
¼ teaspoon cumin
1/8 teaspoon sea salt
1/8 teaspoon garlic powder

Combine all ingredients. Serve on beef burgers, veggie burger or fish. Store leftovers in glass jar with lid and refrigerate. Yield: 4 servings.

## TRI COLOR SALSA

1 large red bell pepper, seeded and chopped
1 large green bell pepper, seeded and chopped
2 cups peeled and diced red, ripe tomatoes
1 sweet onion chopped
½ teaspoon salt
½ teaspoon freshly ground black pepper
Juice of 1 lemon

Mix all the ingredients, together, cover and chill in the refrigerator until ready to serve. Excellent served as a condiment with roast beef, fajitas or as a dip with blue corn tortilla chips.  Yield: Approximately 2 cups

## OLIVE CHEESE SPREAD

4 oz. reduced fat cream cheese
½ cup light mayonnaise
½ cup chopped green olives stuffed with pimentos
1 cup shredded Monterey Jack & Colby cheese blend

Let cream cheese soften at room temperature.  Beat with electric mixer until smooth. Beat in mayonnaise and mix well. Add chopped olives and shredded cheese.  Beat until thoroughly mixed.  Spoon into a pint size wide mouth jar with lid and store in refrigerator until ready to serve.  Yield: 1 pint. Serve with crackers.

BEVERAGES

## LEMON QUENCHER
5 cups water divided
1 cup lemon juice
2/3 cup honey
1 cup sugar
2 teaspoons grated lemon peel
Ice cubes

In a blender combine lemon juice, water, honey and lemon peel. Stir until blended. Cover and refrigerate for at least 2 hours. Serve over ice.

## FRESH LEMONADE SYRUP
3 cups sugar
1 cup boiling water
3 cups lemon juice (about 16 lemons)
2 tablespoons grated lemon peel

In a 1-1/2 quart heat-proof container, dissolve sugar in boiling water. Cool. Add lemon juice and peel, mix well. Cover and store in the refrigerator for up to 1 week or place in freezer containers and freeze. Yield: 5-1/2 cups syrup.
To prepare lemonade: For 1 serving, combine ¼ to 1/3 cup syrup and ¾ cup cold water in a glass, stir well. For 8 servings, combine 2-2/3 cups syrup and 5 cups cold water in a 2 qt. pitcher; stir well.

## CLASSIC LEMONADE

1 cup sugar
3 cups water
1 cup fresh lemon juice
In a small saucepan, bring sugar and 1 cup water to a boil stirring to dissolve sugar. Simmer 5 minutes. Let cool; refrigerate syrup until chilled. In a pitcher, mix remaining 2 cups water, the lemon juice and chilled syrup. Serve in tall glasses over ice.

## EGGNOG
4 eggs
1 cup heavy whipping cream
4 cups milk
1 teaspoon vanilla
1 teaspoon nutmeg

Mix all together and chill

# BREADS, ROLLS & MUFFINS

## BLUEBERRY-ORANGE BREAD

2 cups unbleached all-purpose flour
1 teaspoon Rumford baking powder
½ teaspoon sea salt
½ teaspoon baking soda
2 tablespoons butter, cut up
¼ cup boiling water
1 egg slightly beaten
1 cup sugar
½ cup fresh orange juice
1 cup blueberries

Grease the bottom and ½ inch up the sides of a loaf pan, set aside. Preheat oven to 350 Degrees. In a large bowl, stir together flour, baking powder, salt and soda; make a well In center and set aside. Stir together butter and boiling water until butter is melted.

In a medium bowl, combine egg, sugar, and orange juice; stir in butter mixture. Add to the dry ingredients, stirring just until moistened. Fold in blueberries. Spoon the batter Into the prepared pan. Bake in preheated oven about 60 minutes or until a toothpick inserted near the center comes out clean. Cool for 10 minutes. Remove loaf from pan. Cool completely. Wrap in foil and store overnight. Makes 1 loaf (16 slices.)

# YOGURT CORN BREAD

¾ cup cornmeal
¾ cup unbleached all-purpose flour
1 tablespoon sugar
1-1/2 teaspoons Rumford baking powder
½ teaspoon baking soda
½ teaspoon sea salt
1 egg
1 cup nonfat plain yogurt
2 Tbsp. skim milk or soy milk
3 Tbsp. canola oil

Preheat oven to 425 degrees. Coat an 8-inch square baking pan with cooking spray. In a large bowl, mix the cornmeal, flour, sugar, baking powder, baking soda and salt until blended. In a small bowl using a whisk, blend the egg with the yogurt, milk and oil until smooth. Stir the yogurt mixture into the dry ingredients and whisk gently, until the batter has no lumps. Pour into the pan and smooth the top with a spoon or spatula. Bake in the center of the oven until it is golden brown on top and begins to pull away from the sides of the pan, about 20 minutes. Cut into 12 squares and serve hot.

# EGGNOG CHERRY NUT BREAD

2-1/2 cups unbleached all-purpose flour
1 cup sugar
3-1/2 teaspoons Rumford baking powder
1 teaspoon sea salt
1-1/4 cups eggnog
1 egg
3 Tbsp. canola oil
½ cup chopped salad cherries
1 cup walnuts

Heat oven to 350 degrees. Grease bottom of loaf pan only.
Beat all ingredients except nuts and cherries in large bowl on
low speed until mixed. Beat on medium speed for
30 seconds scraping bowl often. Stir in nuts & drained
cherries. Pour into pan and bake 60-65 minutes or until
toothpick inserted in middle comes out clean. Immediately
Remove from pan.

## ZUCCHINI BREAD

3 eggs
1-2/3 cup sugar
1 cup canola oil
1-1/2 teaspoons vanilla extract
3 cups unbleached all-purpose flour
1 teaspoon Rumford baking powder
1 teaspoon baking soda
1 teaspoon sea salt
1 teaspoon ground nutmeg
1 teaspoon cinnamon
¾ cup chopped walnuts
2 cups zucchini, coarsely shredded
1 cup seedless raisins

Beat eggs until light. Thoroughly beat in next three
ingredients. Stir dry ingredients together. Add to egg-oil-
sugar mixture and beat until smooth. When well blended,
Stir in remaining ingredients. Place batter in two greased and
floured loaf pans (8-1/2" x 4-1/4".) Bake at 350 degrees for 1
hour.

# SPELT YEAST BREAD

2-1/2 cups water, warmed to 115 degrees
½ cup thawed apple juice concentrate, warmed to 115 degrees
2 packages quick rise yeast
2 teaspoons sea salt
¼ cup oil
9 cups spelt flour, divided

Combine the water, juice and yeast in a large electric mixer bowl and let the mixture stand for about 10 minutes or until foamy.  Add 4-1/2 cups of the spelt flour and beat on medium speed for 5 to 8 minutes. (During this time the gluten in the dough will develop into long strands and begin to climb up the beaters.)  Beat in the oil and salt.  Stir in another 1 to 2 cups of spelt flour.  Put the dough on a floured board and knead it for 10 minutes, kneading in enough of the remaining flour to make a firm and elastic dough.  Put the dough into an oiled bowl and turn it once so that the top of the ball is also oiled. Cover it with a towel and let it rise in a warm (85 to 90 degrees) place until it has doubled in volume, about 45 minutes to 1 hour.  Punch down the dough and shape into 2 oiled 9" x 5" loaf pans.  Let the loaves rise until they have doubled again, about 45 minutes.  Bake at 375 degrees for 40 to 45 minutes.  Immediately run a knife around the edges of the loaves and remove them from the pans.  Cool them on a wire rack.

## CRUSTY CHEESE BREAD

4 Tbsp. butter, softened
½ teaspoon garlic powder
Pinch of white or black pepper
½ loaf French bread (8 oz.) cut in half
1 cup shredded mozzarella cheese, 3 cheese combination or Parmesan cheese

In a small bowl, combine the butter, garlic powder and pepper. Cut ½ of loaf into serving size pieces, saving other half for something else. Spread butter mixture over bread slices and sprinkle with cheese. Place on an ungreased baking sheet. Bake at 350 degrees for 11 minutes. Yield: 6 slices

## BUTTERMILK ORANGE MUFFINS

1 stick (1/2 cup butter), softened
2/3 cup sugar
2 teaspoons Rumford baking powder
¼ teaspoon baking soda
¼ teaspoon sea salt
2 teaspoons grated orange peel
2 large eggs
2/3 cup low-fat buttermilk
2 cups unbleached all-purpose flour
Heat oven to 400 degrees. Fill twelve 2-1/2 inch muffin pans with paper liners. In a large bowl, with mixer on medium speed, beat butter, sugar, baking powder, baking soda, salt and orange peel until blended. Beat in eggs, then buttermilk, until blended (batter will look curdled.) Stir in flour just until blended (don't over mix.) Divide batter among muffin cups. Bake 16 to 20 minutes until a wooden pick inserted in centers comes out clean. Cool in pan on wire rack 5 minutes, then invert on rack, turn top side up and cool completely.

## BLUEBERRY MUFFINS

2 cups unbleached all-purpose flour
2/3 cup sugar
1 Tbsp. Rumford baking powder
½ teaspoon sea salt
2 eggs
1 cup milk
1/3 cup butter, melted
1 teaspoon ground nutmeg
1 teaspoon vanilla extract
2 cups fresh blueberries

In a mixing bowl, combine flour, sugar, baking powder and salt. In another bowl, beat eggs. Blend in milk, butter, nutmeg and vanilla; pour into dry ingredients and mix just until moistened. Fold in blueberries. Fill greased or paper-lined muffin cups two-thirds full. Bake at 375 degrees for 20-25 minutes. Yield: 12 muffins

## CORN MUFFINS

1-1/2 cups unbleached all-purpose flour
1 cup yellow cornmeal
½ cup sugar
1 tablespoon Rumford baking powder
¾ teaspoon sea salt
½ cup butter (1stick), melted
2 large eggs
¾ cup low fat milk
2 Tbsp. honey
2 Tbsp. maple syrup

Preheat oven to 375 degrees. Grease well 12 standard muffin-pan cups. In a large bowl, mix flour, cornmeal, sugar, baking powder, and salt. Stir in butter until blended. In a small bowl, whisk eggs, milk, honey and maple syrup until mixed. Stir egg mixture into flour mixture just until combined (batter will be lumpy). Spoon batter into muffin cups. Bake muffins 20 to 22 minutes or until toothpick inserted in center of muffin comes out clean. Cool muffins in pan on wire rack 10 inutes. With tip of knife, loosen muffins from pan and remove; serve warm.

# RAISIN BRAN MUFFINS

1-1/4 cups unbleached all-purpose flour
3 teaspoons Rumford baking powder
½ teaspoon sea salt
½ cup sugar
3 cups Raisin Bran
1-1/4 cups milk
1 egg
½ cup vegetable or canola oil

Stir together flour, baking powder, salt and sugar. Set aside.
Measure Raisin Bran & milk into mixing bowl. Stir to
combine. Let stand 1 to 2 minutes or until cereal is softened.
Add egg and oil. Beat well. Add dry ingredients to cereal
mixture, stirring only until combined. Portion batter evenly
into 12 greased 2-1/2 inch muffin pan cups. Bake in oven at
400 degrees F, about 25 minutes or until muffins are golden
brown. Serve warm. Yield: 12 muffins

## FRENCH BREAKFAST PUFFS

1-1/2 cups unbleached all-purpose flour
½ cup sugar
1/8 teaspoon sea salt
1-1/2 teaspoons Rumford baking powder
¼ teaspoon ground nutmeg
1 egg
½ cup milk
1/3 cup melted butter
¼ cup sugar & ½ teaspoon ground cinnamon
1/3 cup melted butter

In a mixing bowl combine flour, ½ cup sugar, baking powder, nutmeg, and 1/8 teaspoon salt. Make a well in the center. In another bowl beat egg slightly; stir in milk and 1/3 cup melted butter. Add egg mixture to flour mixture. Stir just until moistened (batter may be lumpy.) Lightly grease muffin cups. Fill cups 1/3 full with batter. Bake in a 350 degree oven for 20-25 minutes or until golden. Combine remaining sugar & cinnamon. Dip hot muffins in melted butter and then in the sugar cinnamon mixture until coated.

## BLENDER WAFFLES

2 cups unbleached all-purpose flour
3 teaspoons Rumford baking powder
¼ teaspoon sea salt
1 teaspoon sugar
2 eggs
1-1/2 cups milk
¼ cup vegetable or canola oil

Place eggs, milk, and oil in blender. Cover and run on high speed until creamy (about) 30 seconds. Add remaining ingredients and mix at high speed until smooth (1-1/2 minutes.) Preheat electric waffle iron. Pour mixture onto hot waffle grid. Bake until golden brown.

## CHEESE WAFFLES

2 cups unbleached all-purpose flour
4 teaspoons Rumford baking powder
1 Tbsp. sugar
½ teaspoon sea salt
2 eggs
1-1/3 cups milk
½ cup butter, melted
1 cup shredded cheddar cheese

Heat waffle iron. Beat eggs with electric beater until fluffy; beat in remaining ingredients just until smooth. Stir in cheese until well mixed. Pour batter from cup or pitcher onto center of hot waffle iron. Bake until steaming stops, about 5 minutes. Remove waffle carefully.

## MADE FROM SCRATCH WAFFLES

2-1/4 cups unbleached all-purpose flour
1-1/2 teaspoons Rumford baking powder
1 teaspoon sea salt
1 Tbsp. sugar
3 eggs, separated
1-1/2 cups milk
3/8 cup butter, melted

In a medium sized bowl, combine the flour, baking powder, salt and sugar. Combine egg yolks, milk and butter in a small bowl and stir into dry ingredients just until moistened.
In a small mixing bowl, beat egg whites until soft peaks form; gently fold into batter.

Bake in a preheated waffle iron that has been sprayed with cooking spray and waffles are golden brown.

Yield: 4-6 servings

## OATMEAL PANCAKES

1 egg beaten
¾ cup unbleached all-purpose flour
1 Tbsp. sugar
2 teaspoons Rumford baking powder
½ teaspoon baking soda
½ teaspoon sea salt
½ cup quick oatmeal
1 cup buttermilk or plain low-fat yogurt
2 tablespoons canola oil

Preheat griddle until a few drops of water "dance" on the service. Spray with cooking spray. Mix dry ingredients. Beat egg and stir in buttermilk. Add all at once to dry ingredients. Pour batter onto griddle to make four pancakes and turn when bubbles pop. Remove from pan when second side is browned.

## GREAT PANCAKES

1 egg beaten
1 cup plain low fat yogurt
1-1/4 cups unbleached all-purpose flour
2 teaspoons Rumford baking powder
½ teaspoon baking soda
½ teaspoon sea salt
¼ cup unsweetened applesauce
1 Tbsp. sugar

Mix dry ingredients. Beat egg and add yogurt. Add all at once to dry ingredients with ¼ cup of applesauce. Place on preheated griddle making 4 pancakes at one time.

## SWEET POTATO PANCAKES

Original recipe by Laura A. Reynolds

1. **Mash**   ½ cup cooked sweet potato
   ½ cup large banana

2. **Add**   3 beaten eggs (or equiv. amount egg substitute)
   ¼ to ½ cup wild rice, cooked (optional)
   ½ teaspoon cinnamon
   1/8 teaspoon cloves
   1/8 teaspoon ginger
   1 teaspoon vanilla
   1-1/2 cups buttermilk
   1 Tbsp. safflower/canola oil

3. **Sift**   1 cup flour (all purpose or spelt)
   ¼ cup cornmeal
   ½ teaspoon salt
   1 teaspoon baking powder
   1 teaspoon baking soda
   1 Tbsp. sugar

4. Stir mixture 3 into mixture 2, just enough to moisten

5. Preheat griddle until a few drops of water "dance" on the surface. Spray griddle with cooking oil spray, plain or butter flavor. Pour batter onto griddle to make 4"cakes, turn when bubbles pop. Remove from griddle when 2nd side is browned; place on plate in warm oven until all batter is uses. Serve.

Note: If you prefer to use only part of batter, you can freeze the rest & use at a later date, adding additional liquid (water/milk) if needed to attain consistency.

## CREPES SUZETTE

1 cup unbleached all-purpose flour
¼ teaspoon sea salt
2 Tbsp. sugar
½ teaspoon cinnamon
1 cup milk
2 eggs, slightly beaten
2 Tbsp. melted butter or margarine

Sift flour, salt, sugar and cinnamon together. Add milk and butter to eggs. Beat with a rotary beater until smooth. Heat large (10 inch) frying pan with 1 Tbsp. oil. Use six tablespoons in heated frying pan for one crepe smoothing out to edge of pan. Brown on both sides. Remove from pan and keep warm. Serve with maple syrup. Yield: 3 large crepes. Double recipe for 6 crepes.

## CREPES SUZETTE-LOW FAT VERSION

¾ cup 2% milk
½ cup unbleached all-purpose flour
1 Tbsp. sugar
1/8 teaspoon sea salt
1 egg white
Nonstick Cooking Spray

Mix flour and sugar. Beat egg white with milk. Pour into flour mixture and beat with rotary beater until smooth. Serve with Orange Sauce or maple syrup.

## ORANGE SAUCE

¼ teaspoon finely shredded orange peel
1/3 cup orange juice
1/3 cup light corn syrup
2 Tbsp. butter or margarine
Cook and stir just until bubbly. Yield: 4 servings

## MADE FROM SCRATCH BISCUITS

2 cups unbleached all-purpose flour
3 teaspoons Rumford baking powder
1 teaspoon sea salt
½ teaspoon garlic powder
2/3 cup milk
1/3 cup canola oil

Mix flour, baking powder, salt and garlic powder in bowl. Pour 2/3 cup of milk into glass measuring cup. Add enough canola oil to make 1 cup. Make a well in center of dry ingredients. Pour in milk and oil. Mix with a fork until dough forms. Knead dough on waxed paper until smooth. Cut with a floured biscuit cutter and place on ungreased baking pan. Bake at 450 degrees for 10-12 minutes. Yield: 8 biscuits

## BUTTERMILK BISCUITS

Follow recipe above except substitute 2/3 cup of buttermilk for regular milk. Decrease baking powder to 2 teaspoons and add ½ teaspoon of baking soda. Bake at 450 degrees for 10-12 minutes. Yield: 8 biscuits

Note: Add ½ cup of shredded cheddar cheese to either recipe for cheese biscuits

# RYE BREAD LAURA

1-1/2 cups warm water
2 pkg. (2 Tbsp.) dry yeast
1 Tbsp. sugar
½ cup molasses
2 teaspoons salt
2 Tbsp. soft butter
2-1/2 cups stone ground rye flour
2-3 cups spelt flour
Finely grated rind of 1 large or 2 small oranges
2 Tbsp. Caraway seeds
Cornmeal

In a mixing bowl dissolve yeast in warm water with 1 Tbsp. sugar. Blend in molasses, butter, salt and orange rind. Stir in rye flour and caraway seeds. Add enough of spelt flour to handle easily. Place in greased bowl, turning so all sides will be greased. Cover with damp cloth and put in warm place to rise until about double in size. Return to board, shape into 2 round loaves. Place on slightly greased cookie sheet sprinkled with corn meal. Cover with damp cloth & let rise about 1 hour. Bake in preheated oven 30-40 minutes at 375 degrees until brown.
Recipe by Laura A. Reynolds

# CANDY

## CHOCOLATE FUDGE

1 jar (7 oz.) marshmallow crème
2/3 cup fat free evaporated milk
½ cup butter, cubed
2 teaspoons vanilla extract
3 cups (18 oz.) semisweet chocolate chips
2 cups walnuts chopped

Line a 9 inch square pan with heavy duty foil and coat with cooking spray, set aside.

In a large saucepan, combine the marshmallow crème, evaporated milk and butter.

Cook & stir over medium heat until smooth.  Bring to a boil and boil for 5 minutes. Remove from heat and stir in chocolate chips, nuts and vanilla.  Pour into prepared pan and refrigerate for 2 hrs. or until firm.  Using foil remove from pan.  Cut into 1 inch squares.  Store in refrigerator.

## WALNUT FUDGE

1 can (14 oz.) sweetened condensed milk
12 ounces semisweet chocolate, chopped or 12 oz. of chocolate chips and 2 ounces unsweetened chocolate, chopped
1-1/2 teaspoons of vanilla extract
1/8 teaspoon sea salt
1 cup walnuts, chopped

Line an 8"x 8" baking pan with foil.  In 3-quart saucepan, combine condensed milk and chocolates.  Cook over medium low heat 5 minutes or just until chocolates melt and mixture is smooth, stirring constantly.  Remove saucepan from heat, stir in vanilla, salt and walnuts.  Pour chocolate mixture into prepared pan; spread evenly.  Refrigerate until firm, at least 1 hour or overnight.  Invert fudge onto cutting board; discard foil.  Cut fudge into 8 strips, and then cut each strip crosswise into 8 squares.  Store in a tightly covered container, layering with waxed paper. Fudge will keep up to one week at room temperature or one month if refrigerated.

## ALMOND & CHERRY BARK

Prep: 20 minutes plus chilling
¾ cup natural almonds, toasted and chopped
¾ cup dried tart cherries
12 ounces semisweet chocolate, chopped
8 ounces white chocolate, chopped

In a small bowl, combine almonds and cherries and set aside. In a 2-quart saucepan, melt semisweet chocolate over low heat, stirring. In a 1 quart saucepan, melt white chocolate over low heat, stirring. Remove saucepans from heat. Stir half of almond mixture into semisweet chocolate. On large cookie sheet, spread semisweet-chocolate mixture to about ¼ inch thickness. Drop white chocolate by tablespoons onto semisweet chocolate mixture. With tip of knife, swirl chocolates together for marbled look. Sprinkle with remaining almond mixture. Refrigerate 1 hour or until firm. Break bark into pieces. Store in refrigerator up to 1 month.

Yield: 2-1/2 lbs.

# TROPICAL FRUIT JELLIES

Prep: 5 minutes plus standing overnight
1 box (1-3/4 oz.) Sure Jell powdered fruit pectin (no substitutions)
¾ cup tropical fruit juice blend
½ teaspoon baking soda
¾ cup light corn syrup
1 cup plus 6 Tbsp. sugar
2 drops yellow and 1 drop red food coloring (optional)
Line 8"x 8" metal baking pan with foil. Spray foil with nonstick cooking spray.

 In 2-quart saucepan, mix pectin, juice, and baking soda (mixture will be foamy.)  In 2 quart saucepan, mix corn syrup and 1 cup sugar.  Place both saucepans over high heat at the same time, stirring both mixtures frequently.  Cook about 4 minutes or until foam thins from pectin mixture and sugar mixture come to a full rolling boil (a boil that does not stop bubbling when stirred.)  Gradually add pectin mixture to boiling sugar mixture, stirring constantly.  Boil 1 minute stirring.  Remove saucepan from heat; stir in food colorings, if using.  Immediately pour mixture into prepared pan.  Let stand at room temperature 4 hours or overnight until firm. Sprinkle waxed paper with 2 Tbsp. sugar.  Invert candy onto waxed paper; discard foil. Sprinkle top of candy with 2 more Tbsp. sugar.  Cut candy into 6 strips, then cut each strip crosswise into 6 squares.  Add 2 more Tbsp. of sugar to waxed paper. Gently toss candy squares in sugar to coat all sides. Place candies on wire rack; Let stand overnight, uncovered, at room temperature.  Store in tightly covered container, with waxed paper between layers, at room temperature, up to 2 weeks. For gift giving, toss candies with additional sugar to coat if necessary.  Arrange in candy papers.

## CHOCOLATE-RAISIN CLUSTERS

1 package (8 squares) Semi-sweet chocolate
1-1/2 cups Raisin Bran

Partially melt chocolate over very low heat. Remove from heat. Stir rapidly until entirely melted. Add cereal and mix lightly until completely coated with chocolate.
Drop from teaspoon onto waxed paper. Chill until chocolate is firm. Yield: 2 dozen

## CHURCH WINDOWS

Melt & cool:
1 stick butter
1-12 oz. package semi-sweet chocolate chips
Add:
1 package colored marshmallows (Use Kraft)
1 cup chopped walnuts

Roll on waxed paper. Chill until firm. Slice and serve. Keep remainder in refrigerator.

Note: For a different flavor, try mint semi-sweet chocolate chips in place of regular ones.

# CHOCOLATE CHERRY FUDGE

1-1/2 cups sugar
2/3 cup evaporated milk (5 fluid ounces)
2 tablespoons butter
¼ teaspoon sea salt
2 cups miniature marshmallows
10 oz. pkg. or 1-1/2 cups dark chocolate chips
¾ cup dried cherries, coarsely chopped
1 teaspoon vanilla extract

Line an 8" square pan with foil. Combine sugar, evaporated milk, butter and salt in saucepan. Bring to full rolling boil over medium heat stirring constantly. Boil, stirring constantly for 4-5 minutes and then remove from heat. Stir in marshmallows, chocolate chips, dried cherries and vanilla. Stir vigorously for 1 minute or until marshmallow are melted. Pour into prepared pan and refrigerate for 2 hrs.

## CASSEROLES AND BRUNCH DISHES

### HASH BROWN QUICHE

3 cups Simply Potato Hash brown potatoes
1/3 cup butter, melted
1 cup diced fully cooked ham
1 cup (4oz.) shredded sharp cheddar cheese or Swiss cheese
¼ cup chopped Vidalia onion
3 eggs
½ cup milk
½ teaspoon sea salt
¼ teaspoon white pepper

Press hash browns between paper towels to remove excess moisture. Press into bottom and sides of an ungreased deep 10 inch pie plate. Drizzle with butter. Bake at 425 degrees for 25 minutes. Combine ham, cheese and onion, spoon over crust. In a small bowl, beat eggs, milk, salt and pepper. Pour over all. Reduce heat to 350 degrees and bake 25-30 minutes or until a knife inserted near the center comes out clean. Allow to stand for 10 minutes before cutting.

Yield: 6 servings

# MACARONI AND CHEESE

2 Tbsp. butter
2 Tbsp. unbleached all-purpose flour
1 teaspoon sea salt
2-1/2 cups low fat milk
2 cups sharp or extra sharp cheddar cheese, grate ¾ of it, slice
remainder
8 ounces elbow macaroni

Heat water in a 3 quart saucepan until boiling. Add macaroni
and cook about 7 minutes stirring occasionally to keep
macaroni from sticking. Remove from heat and drain. In a
large frying pan, melt 2 Tbsp. butter. Remove from heat and
stir in flour and salt. Stir in milk until mixture is smooth.
Return to heat and cook stirring constantly over medium-
high heat until mixture becomes thick. Add all the shredded
cheese and stir until cheese is melted. Put the drained
macaroni in a large casserole dish that has been sprayed with
cooking spray. Stir in sauce mixing until coated. Slice
remaining cheese and place on top. Bake in a 375 degree oven
for 25 minutes.

Yield: 6 servings

# SUMMER SQUASH CASSEROLE

3 small yellow squash, sliced
3/8 cup chopped onion
¾ teaspoon sea salt, divided
2 eggs
1/3 cup mayonnaise
3 teaspoons sugar
Pepper to taste
1/3 cup sharp cheddar cheese
3 Tbsp. crushed cornflake crumbs
1 Tbsp. butter, melted

In a small saucepan combine squash, onion and ¼ teaspoon salt. Cover with water. Bring to a boil. Reduce heat; simmer uncovered, for 2 minutes or until squash is crisp-tender. Drain. In a bowl, beat egg, mayonnaise, sugar, pepper and remaining salt until blended. Stir in cheese and squash mixture. Transfer to greased 11" x 8-1/2"x 2" casserole dish. Toss top with cornflakes and sprinkle butter over all. Bake uncovered at 350 degrees for 25-30 minutes or until golden brown and bubbly.

Yield: 3 servings

## TUNA CASSEROLE

1-1/2 cups noodles
1-7oz. can albacore tuna
1 can Healthy Request Cream of Mushroom soup (10-3/4 ox.)
½ cup milk
1 cup shredded cheddar cheese
1/3 cup chopped sweet onion

Cook noodles in boiling water until tender. Drain. Spray a
medium sized casserole dish with cooking spray. Add tuna
and flake with fork. Combine soup and milk in a small bowl.
Add to tuna along with cheese and onions. Add noodles and
stir to mix completely. Bake at 425 degrees oven for 20 to 25
minutes or until bubbly. Yield: 3 servings

## HEALTHY SCRAMBLED EGGS

½ cup ham diced or bacon crumbled
¼ cup chopped organic celery
¼ cup chopped sweet onion
2 teaspoons butter
4 eggs and ½ cup water
¼ teaspoon black pepper
¼ teaspoon paprika
4 Tbsp. part skim mozzarella cheese
Melt butter in frying pan and add ham, celery and onion.
Cook for 2 minutes. If using bacon, add after cooking celery
and onion. Beat eggs, add water and stir. Pour over
vegetables and add pepper and paprika. Cook until partially
set and scramble. Add cheese and let it melt. Serve over
toasted English muffin or with toast. Yield: 3 servings

## RAPID RAVIOLI

2-9 oz. packages of fresh cheese ravioli
1 Tbsp. olive oil
4 Italian Sausage links
1-26 oz. spicy red pepper pasta sauce
¼ cup chopped fresh basil
Grated Parmesan cheese
Cook ravioli following package directions; drain. In saucepan, in oil, brown sausages, 5 minutes. Add sauce; partially cover; simmer until sausages are cooked, about 8 minutes.
Remove sausages; slice; add to sauce. Spoon over ravioli. Sprinkle with basil. Serve with Parmesan cheese.

## SPINACH QUICHE

1 deep dish 9 inch pie pastry
4 eggs
1 pkg. frozen chopped spinach
1 can evaporated skim milk (1-2/3 cup)
2 cups shredded Swiss cheese
½ teaspoon sea salt
1/8 teaspoon nutmeg

Cook spinach, drain and pat dry. Put in bottom of unbaked pie crust. Spread grated Swiss cheese over top. Beat eggs and milk with salt and nutmeg. Pour into pie shell and bake at 350 degrees for 45 minutes or until a knife inserted in center comes out clean.

# EGGPLANT PARMIGIANA

1 eggplant (12 to 16 oz.) peeled
1 cup fine breadcrumbs
2 Tbsp. butter
1 egg, beaten with 1 Tbsp. 2% milk
Cooking spray
1-8 oz. can tomato sauce (no salt added)
¼ cup chicken broth (low sodium, no MSG)
1 cup shredded low-fat mozzarella cheese
2 Tbsp. grated Parmesan cheese
½ teaspoon garlic powder
½ teaspoon oregano leaves

Cut eggplant crosswise into ½ inch thick slices. In a shallow soup bowl, toss together bread crumbs and melted butter. Place egg and milk in a small shallow bowl and beat with a fork. Dip eggplant slices in egg mixture and then in breadcrumbs turning to lightly coat both sides. Place on large baking sheet that has been sprayed with cooking spray. Bake at 450 degree oven for 15 minutes, turning after halfway through. Remove eggplant from oven. Reduce temperature to 350 degrees. Pour tomato sauce into an 8 oz. Pyrex glass measuring cup. Add chicken broth and spices. Stir to mix well. Place ½ of tomato sauce mixture into a 13" x 9" baking dish that has been sprayed with cooking spray. Place eggplant slices on top. Pour remaining tomato sauce mixture over top. Add Parmesan and mozzarella cheeses. Bake in oven for 20 minutes.

Yield: 4 servings

# COOKIES, CAKES AND BARS

## BUTTER COOKIES

1 cup butter, softened
1 cup sugar
1 egg
2-1/2 cups unbleached all-purpose flour
2 Tbsp. orange juice
1 Tbsp. vanilla extract
1 teaspoon Rumford baking powder

Combine 1 cup butter, sugar and egg in large mixer bowl.
Beat at medium speed until creamy. Reduce speed to low;
add flour, orange juice, vanilla and baking powder.
Beat until well mixed. Divide dough into thirds; wrap in
plastic food wrap. Refrigerate until firm (2 to 3 hours.) Heat
oven to 400 degrees. In lightly floured surface roll out
dough, one third at a time (keeping remaining dough
refrigerated,) to 1/8-1/4 inch thickness. Cut with 3-inch
cookie cutters. Place 1 inch apart on ungreased cookie
sheets. Bake for 6 to 10 minutes or until edges are lightly
browned. Cool completely.

## FROSTING

4 cups powdered sugar
½ cup butter, softened
3 to 4 Tbsp. milk
2 teaspoons vanilla

In a small mixer bowl combine all frosting ingredients. Beat at
low speed, scraping bowl often, until fluffy (1 to 2 minutes.)
Frost and decorate cookies.

# PEANUT BLOSSOM COOKIES

1 bag (8 oz.) Hershey's Kisses
½ cup shortening
¼ cup creamy Natural peanut butter
1/3 cup packed light brown sugar
1/3 cup sugar
1 egg
2 Tbsp. milk
1 teaspoon vanilla extract
1-1/2 cups unbleached all-purpose flour
1 teaspoon baking soda
½ teaspoon sea salt

Heat oven to 375 degrees. Remove wrappers from Hershey's Kisses. Beat shortening and peanut butter in large bowl until well blended. Add milk and vanilla; beat well. Stir together flour, baking soda and salt; gradually beat into peanut butter mixture. Shape dough into 1-inch balls. Roll in granulated sugar; place on ungreased cookie sheet. Bake 8 to 10 minutes or until lightly browned. Immediately press a Hershey's Kiss into center of each cookie; cookie will crack around edges. Remove from cookie sheet to wire rack. Cool completely.
Yield: About 4 dozen cookies

## BUTTERMILK COOKIES

½ cup butter (no substitutes), softened
1 cup sugar
1 egg
1 teaspoon vanilla extract
2-1/2 cups unbleached all-purpose flour
½ teaspoon baking soda
½ teaspoon sea salt
½ cup buttermilk

In a mixing bowl, cream butter and sugar until light and fluffy. Beat in egg and vanilla. Combine flour, baking soda and salt; add to the creamed mixture alternately with buttermilk and mix well. Drop by rounded Tbsp. 2 inches apart onto greased baking sheets. Bake at 375 degrees for 10-12 minutes or until edges are lightly browned. Cool.

## FROSTING

3 Tbsp. butter, softened
3-1/2 cups powdered sugar
¼ cup milk
1 teaspoon each of vanilla and almond extracts
½ cup finely chopped walnuts

Combine butter, sugar, milk and extracts in a mixing bowl; beat until smooth. Frost cookies; sprinkle with walnuts.
Yield: 3 dozen cookies

# CHOCOLATE CHIP PAN COOKIES

2-1/4 cups unbleached all-purpose flour
1 teaspoon baking soda
1 teaspoon sea salt
1 cup butter, softened
¾ cup packed light brown sugar
¾ cup granulated sugar
1 teaspoon vanilla extract
2 eggs
2 cups (12 oz. pkg.) Semi-sweet chocolate chips
1 cup chopped nuts (optional)

Combine flour, baking soda and salt in small bowl. Beat butter, sugars and vanilla extract in medium size bowl. Add eggs one at a time beating after each addition. Gradually beat in flour mixture. Stir in chocolate chips and nuts. Grease a 15" x 10" jelly-roll baking pan. Spread into prepared pan. Bake at 375 degrees for 20 to 25 minutes or until golden brown. Cool in pan on wire rack. Makes 4 dozen bars.

## NO BAKE COOKIES

2 cups quick cooking oats
½ cup of natural peanut butter
½ cup cocoa
½ cup milk
¼ cup butter
2 cups sugar
1 teaspoon vanilla extract

Measure oats and set aside in bowl.  Measure peanut butter and set aside.  Bring sugar, cocoa, milk and butter to a boil for exactly 1 minute.  Remove from stove.  Add oats, peanut butter and vanilla and stir until mixed.  Drop by spoonful's onto waxed paper one inch apart.

## BROWNIE DROP COOKIES

1 cup sugar
½ cup butter, softened
1/3 cup buttermilk
1 teaspoon vanilla extract
1 egg
2 ounces unsweetened chocolate, melted and cooled
1-3/4 cups unbleached all-purpose flour
1 cup chopped pecans
½ teaspoon baking soda
½ teaspoon sea salt
Heat oven to 400 degrees.  Mix sugar, butter, buttermilk, vanilla, egg and chocolate in medium bowl.  Stir in flour, nuts, baking soda and salt.  Drop dough by rounded teaspoons about 2 inches apart onto ungreased cookie sheet.  Bake 8 to 10 minutes or until almost no indentation remains when touched.  Immediately remove from cookie sheet. Cool and frost with Chocolate Frosting.  Yield: 4-1/2 dozen cookies

## CHOCOLATE FROSTING

2 ounces unsweetened chocolate
2 Tbsp. butter
3 Tbsp. low fat milk
2 cups powdered sugar
1 teaspoon vanilla extract

In a medium sized bowl, mix powdered sugar vanilla and milk. Heat chocolate and butter in small Teflon frying pan over low heat, stirring until melted; remove from heat. Stir into bowl with powdered sugar mixture and beat until smooth.

## GOOD FOR YOU COOKIES

1 cup butter
¾ cup packed light brown sugar
¾ cup granulated sugar
2 eggs
1-1/2 teaspoon vanilla extract
2-1/2 cups unbleached all-purpose flour
½ teaspoon baking soda
½ teaspoon sea salt
1-1/2 cups quick cooking oats
1 cup coarsely chopped walnuts
6 oz. semi-sweet chocolate chips
1 cup raisins
1 cup chopped dates

Cream butter, add sugars and beat well. Add eggs and vanilla and beat well. Add flour, salt and soda alternately until it's mixed thoroughly. Stir in oats, nuts, chocolate chips, raisins and dates. Drop by tablespoonsful on cookie sheet and bake for 13-15 minutes in a 350 degree oven. This dough freezes well and can be sliced later to make fresh cookies. Variation: Add 1 cup of chopped dried apricots or figs in place of dates.

# FRENCH APPLE SQUARES

2-1/2 cups unbleached all-purpose flour
1 cup shortening
2 Tbsp. sugar
1 teaspoon sea salt
1 egg yolk, beaten
2/3 cup milk
2 cups McIntosh apples peeled and sliced plus ¾ cup sugar, &
1-1/2 teaspoons vanilla extract
1 Tbsp. butter
1 beaten egg white

Mix together the flour, shortening sugar and salt. Blend in the
beaten egg yolk with the milk. Roll out one half of the dough
to fit the bottom of a jelly roll pan. Spread with the
apple filling to which you have added the ¾ cup of sugar and
vanilla, dot with butter. Roll out remaining dough and place
it over the layer of apples. Brush with beaten egg white.
Bake at 375 degrees for 35 minutes. Glaze with a thin
powdered sugar icing. Cut into squares and serve.

# MY FAVORITE PEANUT BUTTER COOKIES

1 cup sugar
½ cup natural peanut butter
½ cup butter, softened
1 large egg
1-1/2 cups unbleached all-purpose flour
1 cup lightly salted peanuts chopped
½ teaspoon Rumford baking powder
¼ teaspoon baking soda
¼ teaspoon sea salt

Preheat oven to 350 degrees.

In a large bowl, with mixer at medium speed, beat sugar, peanut butter, and butter until creamy, occasionally scraping bowl with rubber spatula.  At low speed, beat in egg.  Add flour, peanuts, baking powder, baking soda and salt.  Beat just until blended.  With hands, shape dough into 1-inch balls.  Place balls 2 inches apart on ungreased cookie sheet.  With hand dip a 4-tined fork into flour and press across top of each cookie.  Repeat at right angle to flatten each cookie to 1-1/4 inches in diameter. Bake for 14 minutes.

Yield: about 2 dozen cookies

# CRANBERRY PECAN COOKIES

2 cups unbleached all-purpose flour
¾ cup sugar
¾ teaspoon sea salt
½ teaspoon baking soda
¼ cup light olive oil
¼ cup butter, melted
½ cup fresh orange juice
1 egg
1 cup dried cranberries
¼ cup chopped pecans
1-1/4 teaspoons grated orange rind

Heat oven to 400 degrees.
Whisk flour, sugar, salt and baking soda in a small bowl, set aside. In a large bowl, beat olive oil, butter and orange juice on medium speed for 2 minutes. Beat in egg until blended. Add cranberries, pecans, and orange rind. Beat for 1 minute. Drop by heaping tablespoons onto baking sheets sprayed with cooking spray, about 2 inches apart. Bake cookies for 8 to 10 minutes, until firm and golden around edges. Transfer cookies to wire racks to cool completely.

Yield: about 3 dozen cookies.

## BEST BROWNIES

2 squares unsweetened chocolate
6 Tbsp. butter
1 cup sugar
2 eggs
1 teaspoon vanilla extract or flavoring
½ cup unbleached all-purpose flour
½ cup chopped walnuts

Melt chocolate and butter in saucepan on top of stove over very low heat. Remove from heat. Add sugar and beat with a large spoon. Add eggs one at a time, beating after each addition. Add vanilla, flour and nuts. Stir until well mixed. Pour into greased 8" x 8" square baking pan. Bake in oven at 350 degrees for 30 minutes. Double recipe for a 13" x 9" baking pan.

# GINGER COOKIES

1 cup sugar plus extra to roll cookies in
¾ cup butter, softened
1 egg
3 Tbsp. dark molasses
2 cups unbleached all-purpose flour
1 teaspoon baking soda
½ teaspoon sea salt
1-1/2 teaspoons ground ginger
1 teaspoon cinnamon
½ teaspoon allspice

Preheat oven to 350 degrees. In a large bowl, cream sugar with butter until light and fluffy. Mix in egg and molasses. In a medium bowl, stir together flour, baking soda and spices. Add to butter mixture and blend well. Use tablespoon size pieces of dough and roll into balls; roll ball in sugar and place on cookie sheet which has been lightly greased or sprayed with cooking spray. Bake until golden brown, about 10 minutes. Cool on brown or parchment paper. Frost with vanilla frosting. Yield: 2 dozen cookies

# VANILLA FROSTING

2 tablespoons butter, softened
3-4 Tbsp. milk
1 teaspoon vanilla flavoring
2 cups powdered sugar

Mix butter with milk and vanilla. Stir until smooth. Gradually add powdered sugar and stir until well blended.

## 1-2-3-4 CAKE

3 cups sifted cake flour
3-1/2 teaspoons Rumford baking powder
½ teaspoon sea salt
1 cup shortening
2 cups sugar
4 eggs, separated
1 cup milk
1 teaspoon vanilla extract

Sift flour, baking powder, and salt together. Cream shortening and sugar until fluffy. Add egg yolks and beat well. Add milk and dry ingredients alternately. Add vanilla. Beat egg whites until stiff and fold in. Turn into 3 greased and floured 9" x 1-1/2 round layer cake pans. Bake at 350 degrees for 30-35 minutes. Remove from oven, cool 5 minutes and then remove from pans and cool thoroughly. Frost with your favorite frosting.

Note: To make your own cake flour, use unbleached all-purpose flour and decrease each cup of flour by 2 tablespoons and add 2 tablespoon of cornstarch.
Ratio: 1 cup unbleached all-purpose flour less 2 tablespoons
        Add 2 tablespoons cornstarch

# MOLASSES CAKE

1 egg
1 cup granulated sugar
1 cup dark molasses (not blackstrap)
1 cup sour milk
1 teaspoon baking soda
1 teaspoon sea salt
1 teaspoon ginger
½ teaspoon cinnamon
½ teaspoon nutmeg
2 heaping teaspoons shortening
2 cups unbleached all-purpose flour

Combine all ingredients. Pour into greased 13″ x 9″ baking pan. Bake at 375 degrees for approximately 45 minutes. Cake is very moist and even better 2 days old. Frost with vanilla or lemon frosting or serve plain with whipped cream.

## EGGLESS CAKE

1-1/4 cups unbleached all-purpose flour
1/3 cup cocoa
1 teaspoon Rumford baking powder
6 Tbsp. butter or light margarine
1 cup sugar
1 cup skim milk
1 tablespoon white vinegar
1 teaspoon vanilla extract.

Heat oven to 350 degrees. Spray one 13" x 9" baking pan with cooking spray. In bowl, stir flour, cocoa and baking soda. In saucepan melt butter or margarine; stir in sugar. Remove from heat. Add milk, vinegar and vanilla to mixture in saucepan and stir. Add dry ingredients. Whisk until well blended. Pour evenly in pan and bake for 20 minutes or until a toothpick inserted in center comes out clean. Frost.

# BANANA CAKE

¾ cup butter
2-1/4 cups sugar
2 eggs
3 cups cake flour
¾ teaspoon Rumford baking powder
1-1/8 teaspoons baking soda
¾ teaspoon sea salt
1-1/2 cups mashed bananas
1-1/2 teaspoons vanilla flavoring
3/8 cup sour milk

Cream butter until soft. Add sugar and beat gradually until light and creamy. Beat in eggs. Mix flour, baking powder, soda and salt. Prepare mashed bananas and add vanilla and sour milk. Add dry ingredients to butter mixture in 3 parts, alternately with banana mixture, beating until smooth after each addition. Bake in greased 10" tube pan in 350 degree oven for 40 minutes. Make sure cake is done by inserting toothpick close to center and it comes out clean. Invert pan on rack and when cool, remove and sprinkle with powdered sugar or frost.

## SOUR CREAM LOAF

2-1/2 cups unbleached all-purpose flour
1-1/2 teaspoons Rumford baking powder
1/2 teaspoon baking soda
½ teaspoon sea salt
1 container (8 oz.) low fat sour cream
1 teaspoon vanilla extract
1-1/2 cups sugar
½ cup butter, softened
1 Tbsp. grated orange peel
2 large eggs

Preheat oven to 350 degrees. Grease 9" x 5" loaf pan; dust with flour. On waxed paper combine flour, baking powder, baking soda, and salt. In a small bowl, with wire whisk or fork, mix sour cream and vanilla. In large bowl, with mixer at low speed, beat sugar, butter, and orange peel until smooth. Increase speed to high; beat until creamy. Reduce speed to low; add eggs, beating well and scraping bowl occasionally with rubber spatula. Add flour mixture alternately with sour cream mixture, beginning and ending with flour mixture. Spoon batter into prepared pan; spread evenly. Bake 50 to 55 minutes or until toothpick inserted in center of loaf comes out clean. Cool loaf in pan for 10 minutes.

## ORANGE FROSTING

2 Tbsp. butter, softened
1-1/2 cups powdered sugar
3 tablespoons fresh orange juice

Mix butter with powdered sugar and add orange juice as needed. Mix until smooth and creamy. Frost above cake when it has cooled.

## RASPBERRY CREAM FILLING

1 cup heavy whipping cream
¼ cup sugar
1 teaspoon vanilla
½ cup raspberries

Whip cream with sugar and vanilla. Reserve 1 cup frosting; fold ½ cup raspberries into the rest.

Cut above cake in half horizontally. Scoop out the centers, leaving a ½ inch rim. Spread thin layer reserved cream on cut side of bottom half. Fill the centers with raspberry mixture. Replace top. Frost with remaining cream and sprinkle with additional berries. Strawberries can be substituted for raspberries.

## BANANA CUPCAKES

1-1/2 cups unbleached all-purpose flour
¾ teaspoon baking soda
½ teaspoon sea salt
1 cup sugar
¾ cup vegetable or canola oil
3 Tbsp. buttermilk or sour milk
2 large eggs, lightly beaten
1 cup mashed bananas (from 2 large or 3 small)
1 teaspoon vanilla extract

Place flour, baking soda and salt in a large mixing bowl and stir with a fork to combine. Add the sugar and stir to combine. Add the oil, buttermilk, eggs and mashed bananas and stir until the mixture is smooth and just blended, 50 to 60 strokes. Pour the batter into a paper lined cupcake pan. Bake at 350 degrees for 20-25 minutes or until a toothpick inserted in center comes out clean. Yield: 12 large cupcakes
Note: Reduce oil to ½ cup and add 1 extra banana or small cup of unsweetened Applesauce if desired. This recipe can also be made into a 9" square cake. Bake cake for 30 minutes at 350 degrees.

## BAVARIAN FROSTING

Thicken on stove in small non-stick frying pan:
¼ cup milk
1-1/2 Tbsp. flour
Cool:
Beat with mixer, ¼ cup butter, ¼ cup shortening and ½ cup sugar. Add cooled flour mixture and 3 tablespoons powdered sugar. Beat well and add 1 teaspoon vanilla extract. Frost cooled cupcakes. Note: To make chocolate frosting, add 1 tablespoon of dark cocoa

# SOLO STRAWBERRY SHORTCAKE

2 cups unbleached all-purpose flour
3 teaspoons Rumford baking powder
½ teaspoon sea salt
¼ cup sugar
1/3 cup canola oil
1 egg beaten in a 1 cup glass measuring cup
Add enough milk to measuring cup to make 2/3 cup.
Add enough canola oil to make 1 cup liquid in measuring cup.

Mix flour, baking powder, salt and sugar. Make a well and
add measuring cup of liquid. Stir with a fork until it clings
into a ball. Knead dough on waxed paper.

Cut with biscuit cutter that has been dipped in flour. Place on
ungreased baking pan and bake at 450 degrees for 12 minutes
or until lightly browned. Yield: 8-10 servings

To serve: cut the amount of biscuits you are serving in half.
Spread with butter. Place one whole biscuit in each serving
bowl. Clean 1 quart of fresh strawberries. Slice and place in a
2 quart bowl and add ¾ cup of sugar. Mix well.

Place strawberries on bottom half and then replace top,
placing more strawberries on top. Add Cool Whip or
whipped cream to top.

## MINIATURE FRUITCAKES

¾ cup sugar
¼ cup unbleached all-purpose flour
½ teaspoon Rumford baking powder
1/8 teaspoon sea salt
1-1/2 cups chopped walnuts
1 cup chopped dates
¾ cup chopped mixed candied fruit (about 4 ounces)
2 eggs, separated
½ teaspoon vanilla extract
Halved candied cherries

In a bowl, combine the first seven ingredients. Combine egg yolks and vanilla; stir into dry ingredients. In a small mixing bowl, beat egg whites until stiff peaks form; fold into batter. Fill greased and floured muffin cups two-thirds full. Cover the muffin tin tightly with heavy-duty aluminum foil. Bake at 275 degrees for 1 hour. Uncover; top each fruitcake with cherries. Bake 5 minutes longer or until a toothpick inserted near the center comes out clean. Cool for 5 minutes. Run a knife around the edges of each cup; Remove to a wire rack to cool completely. Yield: 1 dozen

Note: Rice, Spelt or any non-gluten flour can be substituted for all-purpose wheat flour.

# VANILLA CUPCAKES

½ cup butter, softened
2/3 cup sugar
1 teaspoon Rumford baking powder
1 teaspoon baking soda
2 eggs
1 teaspoon vanilla extract
2/3 cup buttermilk or plain yogurt
1-1/3 cups unbleached all-purpose flour

Heat oven to 350 degrees. Line 12 muffin cups with paper liners. Beat butter, sugar, baking powder and baking soda in a large bowl with mixer on high speed until well blended. Add egg and vanilla; beat 2 to 3 minutes until fluffy. Reduce mixer speed to low and beat in buttermilk or yogurt (batter will look curdled,) then flour, just until blended. Spoon into muffin cups. Bake 20 to 25 minutes until toothpick inserted in center comes out clean. Cool in pan for 5 minutes, then remove and cool completely. Frost with strawberry frosting.

# STRAWBERRY FROSTING

½ cup butter, softened
4 strawberries, cleaned, cut up and crushed
2-1/2 cups powdered sugar
3-4 Tbsp. milk
1 teaspoon vanilla extract

Mix butter, crushed strawberries, vanilla and powdered sugar. Add enough milk to make it the consistency for spreading.

DESSERTS AND PIES

## VANILLA CORNSTARCH PUDDING

2 cups 2% milk
3 Tbsp. cornstarch
¼ cup sugar
1/8 teaspoon sea salt
1 teaspoon vanilla extract

Mix cornstarch, sugar and salt in 2 quart saucepan. Stir in
milk until completely mixed. Cook on top of stove on medium
heat stirring constantly until mixture boils. Add vanilla
and pour into dessert dishes and cool. Refrigerate.
Yield: 4 servings

## CHOCOLATE PUDDING

1/2 cup unsweetened cocoa
¾ cup sugar
¼ cup plus ½ Tbsp. cornstarch
3 cups 2% milk
1 large teaspoon vanilla

Mix cocoa, sugar and cornstarch in medium sized cooking
pan. Add milk and stir until well mixed. Cook over medium
heat on stove until it becomes thick and starts to boil. Remove
from stove, add vanilla and pour into bowl. Cool and
refrigerate. Serve with whipped cream or whipped topping if
desired. Yield: 4-5 servings

## EGG CUSTARD

3 cups 2% milk
4 Tbsp. butter
½ cup sugar or 5 Tbsp. fructose
½ teaspoon cornstarch
¼ teaspoon sea salt
1 teaspoon vanilla
6 large eggs
Nutmeg to sprinkle on top

Scald milk with butter until butter is all melted. In medium sized mixing bowl beat eggs with sugar or fructose, cornstarch, salt and vanilla. Add scalded milk and stir. Sprinkle top with nutmeg and bake in a boiling water bath (Set bowl in a large roasting pan of hot water.) Bake for 45 degrees at 350 degrees. Check with a sharp knife. If it comes out clean it is done. Remove from water and set bowl on a hot pad to cool. Variation: You may us 1/3 cup of honey instead of sugar. Yield: 8 servings

## RICE PUDDING

1 cup cooked rice
4 eggs
¼ teaspoon sea salt
¼ cup sugar
½ cup raisins
2-1/2 cups scalded milk
1 teaspoon vanilla
¼ teaspoon lemon extract

Beat eggs well, add rice, sea salt, sugar, vanilla and lemon extract. Add milk and mix well. Stir into a 2 qt. bake-proof bowl or casserole dish and bake in a boiling water bath at 400 degrees for 40 minutes.

## RICE PUDDING-RICE COOKER METHOD

Use 1.5 quart Pyrex bowl sprayed with cooking spray
1 cup packed cooked rice
3 eggs beaten
¼ cup sugar
1/4 teaspoon sea salt
1 teaspoon vanilla
2 cups scalded milk

Beat eggs, add sugar, salt and vanilla. Scald milk and add to eggs with rice. Sprinkle nutmeg on top. Place 1 cup hot water in bottom of rice cooker pan. Add 1 tablespoon of vinegar. Place bowl in cooker pan and cover with lid. Cook.

## SLOW COOKER BREAD PUDDING

8 cups cubed day old plain cinnamon rolls
2 cups milk
4 eggs
¼ cup sugar
¼ cup butter
½ teaspoon vanilla extract
¼ teaspoon ground nutmeg
1 cup raisins

Place cubed cinnamon rolls in slow cooker. In mixing bowl, combine next six ingredients. Beat until smooth. Stir in raisins. Pour over cinnamon rolls. Cover and cook on low for 3 hours. Eight slices of cinnamon bread can be substituted for rolls.

## BREAD PUDDING

3 eggs beaten
½ teaspoon sea salt
1 teaspoon ground cinnamon
½ teaspoon ground nutmeg
1-1/2 teaspoons vanilla extract
3 cups milk, scalded
4 Tbsp. butter
¼ cup sugar
3 cups day old French or Homemade White bread
½ cup raisins

Beat eggs in bowl. Add salt, cinnamon, nutmeg and vanilla. Stir in. Scald milk with butter. Add sugar. Pour milk mixture over egg mixture. Cut up bread and place in a casserole dish that has been sprayed with cooking spray. Add raisins and pour liquid mixture over all. Bake in a hot water bath for 1 hour.

## VANILLA YOGURT FREEZE

Cover bottom of paper-lined muffin cups with a Vanilla wafer; top with 2 tablespoon each thawed Cool Whip Lite and strawberry yogurt and one Vanilla wafer stuck halfway in top. Freeze until firm. Use any flavor yogurt for a different taste.

## CHERRY CRISP

2 cups washed, pitted, cut in half fresh sweet cherries
1 cup washed and drained fresh raspberries
¼ cup sugar
1-1/2 Tbsp. cornstarch
½ cup unbleached all-purpose flour
½ cup quick oats
¼ teaspoon sea salt
2-1/2 Tbsp. butter
¼ cup packed light brown sugar

Mix cherries and raspberries with cornstarch and sugar. Place in an 8-inch baking dish sprayed with cooking spray. Bake in a 350 degree oven for 15 minutes. Meanwhile, mix flour, oatmeal, brown sugar and salt in a small mixing bowl. Cut in butter until it resembles small crumbs. After fruit has been baked for 15 minutes, add topping and bake for another 20 minutes.

# PEACH COBBLER

5 cups fresh peaches, peeled and cut into slices
¼ cup sugar
1 Tbsp. fresh lemon juice
1/3 cup butter, softened
¾ cup sugar
1 egg
¾ cup unbleached all-purpose flour
½ teaspoon Rumford baking powder

Preheat oven to 375 degrees. Spray and 8-inch square baking pan with cooking spray.

Layer the peach slices in the pan and sprinkle with sugar and lemon juice. Set aside while making the topping. In a medium mixing bowl, beat butter and sugar with an electric mixer until light and fluffy. Add the egg and beat for 1 more minute. Mix the baking powder with flour and add to butter mixture just until combined. Spoon tablespoons of the batter over the peaches leaving spaces so fruit can bubble around it. Bake 40 minutes or until the top is lightly browned.

## CHERRY COBBLER

1-16 oz. can sour cherries, packed in water
2 Tbsp. quick cooking tapioca
2 Tbsp. light brown sugar
¼ teaspoon ground cinnamon
½ cup unbleached all-purpose flour
¾ teaspoon Rumford baking powder
1/8 teaspoon sea salt
2 Tbsp. butter
¼ cup milk

Preheat oven to 375 degrees.

In small saucepan, combine cherries in water, tapioca, brown sugar, and cinnamon; let sit about 15 minutes or until slightly thickened, stirring occasionally. Into a 9" pie plate pour mixture.

In small bowl, combine flour, baking powder, and salt; mix well. With a knife or pastry blender, cut in the butter until mixture crumbles; stir in milk. Drop dough in 4 mounds over cherries. Bake about 30 minutes or until lightly browned.
Yield: 5 servings

## BEST PECAN PIE

Pastry for 10-inch one crust pie (Use a glass Pyrex deep dish pie plate.)
3 large eggs
2/3 cup sugar
½ teaspoon sea salt
1/3 cup butter, melted
1 cup white corn syrup
1-½ cups broken pecans
1 teaspoon vanilla

Heat oven to 375 degrees. Prepare pastry. Beat egg, sugar, salt, butter and syrup with hand beater. Stir in pecans. Pour into pastry lined pie plate. Bake until set, 40 to 50 minutes. Cool slightly. Serve warm or refrigerate.

Note: While living in Benson, AZ I had pecan trees. I picked the fresh pecans and made these pies and sold them. This is my favorite original recipe.

## CHERRY PIE
Pastry for 2 Crust 9" pie
1-1/2 Tbsp. minute tapioca
1/8 teaspoon sea salt
1 cup sugar
½ cup cherry juice
3 cups water packed red sour cherries or fresh cherries
1/8 teaspoon almond extract

Mix in the order above. Let stand 15 minutes. Pour into greased pie plate that has been lined with pastry. Dot with 1 tablespoon of butter. Put on top crust. Cut slits with a knife in center of pie or cut out a small piece with a cookie cutter before you place top crust on pie. Bake at 350 degrees for 1 hour.

## OLD FASHIONED APPLE PIE

Pastry for 2 Crust 9" pie
1 cup sugar
1 teaspoon ground cinnamon
4 Tbsp. Unbleached all-purpose flour
Dash of sea salt
6 cups thinly sliced apples (Macintosh)
1 teaspoon vanilla extract
2 Tbsp. butter

Place apples in a large mixing bowl. Add sugar, cinnamon, flour, salt and vanilla. Toss to combine and turn into greased, pastry lined deep dish pie plate; dot with butter. Cover with top crust and fold top underneath bottom crust to seal. Cut slits with a knife in center of pie or cut a piece out with a cookie cutter before you place top crust on pie. Bake at 350 degrees for 1 hour.

## BLACKBERRY PIE

Pastry to two crust 9" pie
1 cup sugar
½ cup unbleached all-purpose flour
½ teaspoon ground cinnamon
6 cups fresh blackberries
1 Tbsp. butter

In a large bowl, mix sugar, flour and cinnamon. Stir in blackberries that have been washed and drained. Mix well and spoon into a greased pastry filled pie plate. Cut butter into small pieces and place on top of berries. Cover with top pastry that has slits cut into it in center. Bake at 425 degrees for 15 minutes and then reduce heat to 350 degrees for another 35 minutes or until juice begins to bubble through. Cool on wire rack at least 2 hours.

## BUTTERMILK PASTRY

2 cups unbleached all-purpose flour
1 teaspoon sea salt
2/3 cup shortening
3 Tbsp. butter
2 teaspoons vegetable oil
1/3 cup buttermilk

In a medium bowl, mix flour and salt. Cut in shortening and butter with pastry blender until particles are size of small peas. Mix in oil and buttermilk with fork until all flour is moistened and pastry leaves sides of bowl. Divide in half, shape each half into a ball. Roll pastry with rolling pin on floured pastry cloth and place in a greased 9-inch pie plate. Roll other half and cut out a design with a cookie cutter in center and place over filling.

## PIE CRUST

2 cups unbleached all-purpose flour
1 teaspoon sea salt
¾ cup shortening
6-7 Tbsp. ice water

Blend flour and salt in mixing bowl. Cut shortening into flour mixture using a pastry blender until mixture resembles coarse crumbs with pea size pieces remaining. Add ice water and stir with fork until mixture holds together. Use about 4 tablespoons of ice water at first adding a tablespoon at a time until mixture is just right. Place dough on floured pastry cloth and roll to size. Makes 1-9 inch double crust or 1-10 inch single plus 1 small pie crust. Grease pie plate.

# THREE BERRY PIE

2-12 oz. pkgs. blueberries, washed and drained
1-6 oz. pkg. raspberries
1-6 oz. pkg. blackberries
¾ cup sugar
¼ cup unbleached all-purpose flour
1 Tbsp. butter
½ teaspoon cinnamon
1 Tbsp. lemon juice
Double Crust for 9-inch pie

Mix berries, sugar, flour, cinnamon and lemon juice in a bowl.
Let set for 10-15 minutes. Grease pie plate and place bottom
crust in plate. Add berry mixture and dot with butter.
Before you place top crust onto pie, cut a piece out of the
center with a knife or cookie cutter. After placing top crust
evenly over pie, fold edges underneath bottom crust to
seal. Use a table fork to make lines all around the pie for
decoration. Bake at 350 degrees for 45 minutes. Then raise
temperature to 425 degrees and bake an additional 10 minutes
or until browned.

## LIME CHIFFON PIE

1-1/2 teaspoons unflavored gelatin
¼ cup cold water
1 Tbsp. cornstarch
2/3 cup sugar
¼ teaspoon sea salt
¼ cup fresh lime juice
¼ teaspoon grated lime peel
3 egg whites
1 baked 9″ pastry shell

Soften gelatin in water. Combine cornstarch, 1/3 cup sugar, salt, and lime juice. Bring to a boil and cook over low heat, stirring constantly, until thickened. Remove from heat, add softened gelatin; stir until dissolved. Add grated lime peel, chill till slightly congealed. Beat egg whites till foamy; gradually add remaining 1/3 cup sugar. Beat until mixture stands in soft peaks. Beat gelatin mixture until light. Fold in meringue, then pour into cooled baked pastry shell. Chill till firm. To make Lemon Chiffon Pie: Use lemon juice and grated lemon peel in place of lime.

## CHOCOLATE CHIP BROWNIES

½ cup (1 stick) unsalted butter
2-1 oz. squares unsweetened chocolate
1 cup sugar
½ cup rice flour
½ cup chopped walnuts
½ teaspoon baking powder
1 teaspoon vanilla extract
2 eggs, slightly beaten
1 cup semisweet chocolate chips

Preheat oven to 350 degrees. Spray an 8-inch square pan with cooking spray. Melt the butter and unsweetened chocolate in a medium sized stainless steel cooking pot on a very low heat. Remove from the heat. Add the sugar and then the eggs and mix well. Stir in the flour, nuts, baking powder, and vanilla. Stir in the chocolate chips. Pour the batter into the prepared pan and bake for 30 to 40 minutes, or until a toothpick in the center comes out clean.
Recipe by Laura A. Reynolds

## MEATLOAF

1 egg beaten
2/3 cup milk
1 cup cornflake crumbs
1 cup (4 oz.) shredded Mexican cheese blend
½ cup finely chopped sweet onion
½ cup finely shredded carrot
½ teaspoon sea salt
¼ teaspoon pepper
1 lb. 90% ground beef
¼ cup packed brown sugar
¼ cup ketchup
1 Tbsp. prepared mustard

In a large bowl, combine the first eight ingredients.  Crumble beef over mixture and mix well.  Place in a greased 9" x 5" x 3" loaf pan.

In a small bowl, combine the brown sugar, ketchup and mustard.  Spread over loaf.  Bake at 350 degrees for 60 minutes or until no pink remains.

Let stand 10 minutes before serving.

## ITALIAN STYLE RICE

1 Tbsp. chopped sweet onion
1 Tbsp. butter
½ cup uncooked long grain rice
1 cup reduced sodium chicken broth
1/8 teaspoon ground turmeric
¼ cup shredded Parmesan, Mozzarella, or 5 cheese Italian cheese

In a 10 inch nonstick frying pan, cook onion in butter until tender. Add rice; cook on medium for 2 minutes, stirring constantly. Stir in broth and turmeric; and simmer covered for 20-25 minutes or until liquid is absorbed. Stir in cheese.

Yield: 2 servings

## MEAT, FISH AND FOWL

### STUFFED GREEN PEPPERS

6 green peppers
1 cup cooked long grain white rice
1 lb. 90% ground beef
¼ cup chopped sweet onion
1 teaspoon sea salt
½ teaspoon garlic powder
1 cup low sodium chicken broth

Slice a thin slice across top of peppers. Remove seeds and membranes. Cook peppers in enough water to cover and boil for 5 minutes. Remove and drain. Cook onions in a frying pan with olive oil or cooking spray until yellow. Add ground beef and cook until done. Drain fat. Stir in rice, salt and garlic powder. Add chicken broth and bring to a boil. Remove from stove. Stuff peppers and bake covered for 45 minutes in a 350 degree oven. Remove cover and bake 15 minutes longer.
Yield: 4 to 6 servings

### MOIST MEATLOAF

1-1/2 lbs. 90% ground beef
¾ cup quick cooking oats
2 eggs beaten
¼ cup chopped sweet onion
1 teaspoon sea salt
¼ teaspoon pepper
1 cup tomato or V'8 vegetable juice
Bottled Chili Sauce

Combine all ingredients thoroughly and pack firmly into loaf pan. Spread chili sauce on top. Bake at 350 degrees for 1 hour and 15 minutes. Let stand 5 minutes before serving.

## BEEF PATTIES

1 egg
¼ cup chopped sweet onions
¼ cup plain bread crumbs
1 Tbsp. mustard
1-1/4 lbs. ground beef (Used 93%)
2 pkg's Better than Gravy USDA Organic Gravy Mix for Beef
2 teaspoons prepared horseradish
½ lb. fresh mushrooms, sliced

In a bowl, beat egg, stir in onions, bread crumbs, and mustard.
Crumble beef over mixture and mix well. Shape into four ½
inch thick patties. In a large non-stick skillet (sprayed with
cooking spray), cook patties for 4-5 minutes on each side or
until meat is no longer pink. Meantime, whisk gravy mix
with 2 cups water. Stir on top of stove until it comes to a boil
and is thickened. Take meat patties out of frying pan and keep
warm on a plate. Spray frying pan with cooking spray and
add mushrooms. Cook until tender. Add gravy and patties.
Cook uncovered for 5 minutes. Yield: 4 servings

## SWISS STEAK

12 oz. boneless beef top round steak, tip or chuck steak
3 Tbsp. unbleached all-purpose flour
½ teaspoon sea salt
1/8 teaspoon pepper
2 Tbsp. of vegetable or canola oil
1 can (14-1/2 oz. diced tomatoes)
1 small sweet onion, chopped
1 large green pepper, chopped
½ cup red wine, beef broth or chicken broth
1 teaspoon garlic powder

Cut steak into serving pieces. Combine flour, salt and pepper
in a wide dish. Pound steak in flour mixture on both sides. In
a large skillet, brown steak on both sides in oil. Transfer to
a greased 13" x 9" baking dish. Pour tomatoes, onions, green
pepper, red wine or beef broth and garlic powder over steak.
Cover and bake at 325 degrees for 1-1/2 hrs. or until tender.
Or put in a large plastic cooking bag and place in pan.
Cooking bag bakes faster. Approximately 1 hour, check
periodically after 45 minutes.

# PORCUPINE MEATBALLS

½ cup uncooked long grain rice
½ cup water
1/3 cup chopped sweet onion
½ teaspoon celery salt
½ teaspoon pepper
1/8 teaspoon garlic powder
1-1/2 lbs. lean ground beef (90 or 93%)
1-15 oz. can tomato sauce or 2-8oz. cans
1 cup water
2 Tbsp. brown sugar
2 teaspoons Worcestershire sauce

In a bowl, combine the first six ingredients. Add beef and mix well. Shape into 2-1/2 inch balls. In a large skillet coated with cooking spray, brown meatballs, drain. Combine tomato sauce, water, brown sugar and Worcestershire sauce; pour over meatballs. Reduce heat; cover and simmer for 1 hour. Yield: 6 servings

Note: If you don't have celery salt, use ½ teaspoon of garlic powder instead of the 1/8 teaspoon the recipe calls for.

## CABBAGE ROLLS

1 lb. ground beef
1/3 cup uncooked regular long grain rice
½ teaspoon sea salt
½ teaspoon pepper
½ teaspoon garlic powder
½ cup sweet onion, diced
1 egg
1 head cabbage

Sauce:
Mix two 6 oz. cans tomato sauce and ½ cup low-sodium
chicken broth.

Meat Filling:
Mix ground beef with rice, salt, pepper, garlic powder, onion
and egg.

Roll Preparation:
In a 5 qt. saucepan, heat 4 quarts water to boiling over high
heat. Add cabbage to water; cover and cook for 10 minutes.
Transfer cabbage to colander; when cool enough to handle,
peel off tender outer leaves. Repeat if necessary to obtain 12
large leaves. Trim thick leaves from base of leaves. Place
cabbage leaf in a 1/3 cup measuring cup and stuff with ¼ cup
meat filling trimming overhang if necessary.
Repeat with remaining cabbage leaves and filling. Arrange
cabbage packages seam side down in large baking pan. Spoon
sauce over rolls and cover tightly.

Bake at 325 degrees for 1-1/2 hrs. Check every 20-30 minutes.
Add water if necessary.

# HAWAIIAN MEATBALLS

1 lb. ground round beef
8 oz. can pineapple chunks, juice pack
1-1/2 teaspoons Worcestershire sauce
¼ teaspoon garlic powder
Dash of pepper
½ cup green pepper, cut in 1 inch pieces
1 Tbsp. cornstarch
1 Tbsp. water

Shape meat mixture into 12 balls. Brown in hot skillet about 10 minutes. Drain fat. Drain pineapple and save juice. Add water to juice, to make ¾ cup liquid. Add liquid and seasonings to meatballs. Bring to a boil, reduce heat, cover and cook for 5 minutes. Add pineapple chunks and green pepper. Cook 1 minute longer. Mix cornstarch and water until smooth. Add mixture. Cook until thickened- about 2 minutes. Yield: 4 servings

## CHINESE BEEF AND BEANS

1 lb. top round steak
1 envelope low sodium brown gravy mix
1 Tbsp. soy sauce
½ teaspoon sugar
1/8 teaspoon ground ginger
3 Tbs. canola or vegetable oil
1 pkg. (10 oz. French style green beans thawed) or 1-15-1/2 oz. can of French style green beans
2/3 cup water

Slice steak diagonally into thin strips. Combine contents of gravy mix, soy sauce, sugar and ginger. Pour over meat tossing lightly. Heat half of oil in large skillet. Add beans. Cook and stir 5 minutes until tender crisp. Remove from skillet. Heat remaining oil in same skillet. Add steak and cook 3 to 5 minutes stirring constantly. Add beans and water. Cook, stirring until heated. Serve over hot rice.
Yield: 4 servings

## WIENERS AND SAUERKRAUT

1-14-1/2 to 15 oz. can sauerkraut
2 small gala apples (cored and cut in quarters)
2 to 4 Oscar Mayer Angus Beef Wieners or Kosher
Hot dogs
Hot dog buns

Empty sauerkraut (juice & all) in 1-1/2 qt. saucepan. Place quartered apples on top. Cook over medium heat until it boils. Reduce to simmer, cover and cook for 10 minutes. Add wieners and cook with lid on pan until hot. Wrap buns in paper towel. Microwave for 10 seconds. Serve with mustard and place sauerkraut on top.

# MEATBALLS IN MUSHROOM GRAVY

1 lb. 93% ground beef
¼ cup plain bread crumbs
1 egg
1 can Healthy Request Mushroom Soup
½ cup water
Grated sweet onion
Garlic powder, sea salt and pepper

Mix in a small bowl, Mushroom Soup and ½ cup water.
Combine all ingredients in a bigger bowl and shape into 13
meatballs.  Place in a small roasting pan that has been sprayed
with cooking spray.  Bake at 350 degrees for 15 minutes.
Remove from oven and drain off any grease.  Pour mushroom
soup mixture over meatballs and bake for another 20 minutes.
Yield: 3 servings

# HAM WITH SAUCE

1 bone-in fully cooked ham slice
¼ cup water
1/3 cup strawberry jelly
1 teaspoon prepared horseradish

In a large skillet bring ham and water to a boil.  Reduce heat,
cover and simmer until ham is heated through, turning once.
Meanwhile in a small microwave-safe bowl, combine jelly and
horseradish.  Cover and microwave on high for 2-3 minutes or
until heated through stirring occasionally.  Serve over ham.

Yield: 2 servings

## COUNTRY FRIED STEAK

12 oz. tenderized round steak
1 egg beaten with 1 Tbsp. water
2/3 cup plain bread crumbs
2 Tbsp. Olive oil
Salt & pepper to taste

Cut steak into 4 serving pieces. Beat egg and add water in large soup dish. Add bread crumbs to another soup dish. Dip each piece of steak into egg mixture then pound into bread crumbs making sure each side is well covered. Add olive oil to 10 inch frying pan and heat on medium-high heat. Place meat in olive oil and brown on each side. Reduce heat to medium and then to low turning steaks often. Yield: 4 servings

To make Italian Fried Steak, add 3 Tbsp. grated Parmesan cheese, 1 teaspoon dried oregano, and ¼ teaspoon paprika to breadcrumbs. Cook as directed above.

## CHIPPED BEEF ON TOAST

2 Tbsp. butter
3 Tbsp. unbleached all-purpose flour
4 pkg. Budding Dried Beef or Corned Beef, torn into pieces
3 cups milk
1 cup frozen peas

Melt butter in a 10 inch frying pan. Add pieces of dried beef. Stir until all are curled. Remove from stove; add flour and mix well. Stir in milk and peas. Cook until it comes to a boil and thickens. Serve on buttered toast. Yield: 3 servings

## COUNTRY STYLE SPARE RIBS

1 pkg. Country Style Spare Ribs
1 sweet onion sliced
Sea Salt and pepper to taste
Barbecue Sauce (Used Jack Daniels Honey Smokehouse)

Cook spare ribs in a large frying pan coated with oil. Sprinkle with salt and pepper and brown on each side. Place in a baking pan or small roaster that has been sprayed with cooking spray. Spread with sliced onions and then barbecue sauce. Cover and bake in a 350 degree oven for 1 hr. These are very tender. Yield: 4 servings

## ASIAN BEEF AND NOODLES

1 lb. 90 or 93% lean ground beef
2 pkg. (3 oz. each) Oriental Ramen Noodles, crumbled
2-1/2 cups low sodium Chicken Broth (No MSG)
2 cups frozen cut broccoli
¼ teaspoon ground ginger
2 Tbsp. diced sweet onions

In a large skillet, cook beef over medium-high heat for 4-5 minutes or until no longer pink. Drain off grease. Remove beef from stove, place in a bowl and keep warm. In the same skillet, combine the chicken broth, vegetable, ginger, onions and noodles. Bring to a boil. Reduce heat, cover and simmer for 3-4 minutes or until noodles are tender; stirring occasionally. Return beef to the pan, cook 2-3 minutes or until heated through. This recipe does not use the Seasoning Packets that come with the Ramen noodles. Yield: 4 servings

## BREADED PORK CHOPS

1 egg
1 Tbsp. water
1 cup plain bread crumbs or Cornflake crumbs
2 teaspoons grated Parmesan cheese
1/2 teaspoon onion salt
4 bone-in pork chops

In a bowl, combine egg and water; mix well. In another bowl, combine bread crumbs, Parmesan Cheese and onion salt. Dip chops in egg mixture and then in bread crumb mixture. Place on a greased 11" x 7" baking sheet. Bake uncovered, at 325 degrees for 1 hr. or until juices run clear.

Yield: 4 servings

## GINGERED BEEF STIR-FRY

1 egg white
1 Tbsp. cornstarch
½ teaspoon sugar
¼ teaspoon ground ginger
¼ teaspoon pepper
1 lb. of top round steak (cut into thin strips)
1 Tbsp. canola oil
½ cup chopped green onions
2 Tbsp. reduced-sodium soy sauce
1 pkg. frozen stir-fry vegetables
Hot cooked rice

In a large bowl, whisk egg white, cornstarch, sugar, ginger, pepper and soy sauce until smooth. Add beef and toss to coat; refrigerate covered for 30 minutes. In a large non-stick skillet, heat oil. Sauté onions until crisp-tender. Add beef; stir-fry for 6-7 minutes or until meat is browned. Add vegetables and stir-fry for 4-5 minutes or until vegetables are tender.

## SALMON LOAF

2 small cans "Chicken of the Sea" boneless salmon
1/3 cup celery chopped fine
1/3 cup sweet onion chopped fine
½ cup seasoned Italian bread crumbs (Can substitute cornflake crumbs but add seasonings)
½ cup light mayonnaise

Drain and save liquid from 1 can of salmon only. Flake salmon in a mixing bowl. Add celery and onions to salmon. Combine bread crumbs with liquid. Add mayonnaise and bread crumbs to salmon mixture and mix thoroughly. Place in a small loaf pan and bake at 350 degrees for 45 minutes.

Yield: 4 servings

## CRAB CAKES

¼ cup finely chopped red bell pepper
¼ cup finely chopped green onions
¼ cup light mayonnaise
1 Tbsp. lemon juice
¼ teaspoon seasoned salt
¼ teaspoon garlic powder
Dash of cayenne pepper
2-6 oz. cans "Chicken of the Sea" Crab
1 medium egg beaten
1 cup seasoned bread crumbs
1 Tbsp. butter

In bowl combine red, pepper, green onions, mayonnaise, lemon juice, seasoned salt, garlic powder and cayenne pepper. Stir in Crab, egg and 1/3 cup breadcrumbs (mixture may be sticky). Divide and form mixture into 4 balls. Roll crab balls in remaining breadcrumbs; flatten into cakes about ½ inch thick. In skillet, melt butter over medium heat. Fry crab cakes 3 to 4 minutes per side or until golden brown.

Yield: 4 servings

## BREADED FLOUNDER FILLETS

¼ cup unbleached all-purpose flour
¼ cup cornmeal
½ teaspoon sea salt
½ teaspoon paprika
½ teaspoon pepper
2 egg whites
¼ cup milk
4 flounder fillets
1 Tbsp. grated Parmesan cheese

In a shallow bowl, combine the flour, cornmeal, salt, paprika and pepper. In a shallow bowl, combine egg whites and milk. Coat fish with cornmeal mix then dip into egg white mixture. In a 15" x 10" x 1" baking pan coated with nonstick cooking spray, arrange fish in a single layer. Sprinkle with Parmesan cheese. Bake uncovered at 425 degrees for 8-10 minutes or until fish flakes easily with a fork.

Yield: 4 servings

## SHRIMP SCAMPI

12 oz. bag frozen cooked shrimp (deveined and thawed)
1 Tbsp. olive oil
1 Tbsp. chopped parsley
2 medium green onions chopped or 2 Tbsp. chopped sweet onions
1-14 oz. can low sodium Chicken broth (No MSG)
½ teaspoon garlic powder
Grated Parmesan cheese if desired

Cook onion in oil until soft. Add shrimp, garlic powder and parsley. Stir in chicken broth. Heat thoroughly. Add enough cornstarch until thickened. Serve over fettuccine, angel hair pasta or noodles.

## CHICKEN AND GRAVY

4 skinless, boneless chicken breast halves
3 Tbsp. unbleached all-purpose flour
1 Tbsp. canola oil
1 can of Home Style chicken gravy

Coat chicken with flour. Heat oil in a large skillet over medium heat. Add chicken and cook 15 minutes, turning once, until browned and cooked through. Remove and keep warm. Add gravy to skillet and heat thoroughly. Return chicken to skillet and serve with cooked rice or noodles.

# CHICKEN NUGGETS

1 cup crushed cornflakes (or bread crumbs)
½ cup grated Parmesan cheese
½ teaspoon sea salt
¼ teaspoon black pepper
½ teaspoon garlic powder
½ cup buttermilk
3 boneless chicken breasts cut into 2 inch cubes

Place cornflake or bread crumbs in a shallow bowl.  Add
parmesan cheese, salt, pepper and garlic powder.  In another
shallow bowl pour in buttermilk.  Add chicken pieces to
buttermilk and let soak for about 10 minutes.  Then roll in
crumb mixture and coat well.  Place on pan which has been
sprayed with canola oil cooking spray.  Bake in a 400 degree
oven for 25 minutes.  Halfway through the baking time
remove chicken nuggets from oven and spay all with cooking
spray.  Return to oven and finish baking.  Serve with the
following sweet and sour sauce if desired.  Yield:
4 servings

## Apricot Sweet & Sour Sauce

1 jar of apricot preserves (18 oz.)  Use light preserves for less
sugar. Three to four tablespoons of red wine or cider vinegar.
(Use 1 tablespoon with light preserves.)  White vinegar can
also be used.  Mix until spreading consistency.

## ONE DISH CHICKEN & STUFFING BAKE

2 cups Pepperidge Farm Cornbread Stuffing
3 skinless, boneless chicken breast halves
1 can (10-3/4 oz.) Campbell's Healthy Request Cream of
Mushroom Soup- this is lower in sodium
1/3 cup milk

Mix stuffing, ½ cup boiling water and ½ tablespoon butter.
Spoon stuffing across center of 2 quart shallow baking dish.
Place chicken on each side of stuffing. Mix soup & milk and
pour over Chicken. Bake covered at 400 degrees for 20
minutes. Uncover and bake another 25 minutes or
until chicken is done. Check with fork to see if tender.
Yield: 3 servings

## CHICKEN MARSALA WITH STUFFING AND MUSHROOMS

3 large boneless chicken breasts cut in half
1 box sliced mushrooms (portabella, or white)
1 can Healthy Request Cream of chicken soup
Marsala wine
1/3 cup sour cream
1 box chicken stuffing mix

Cut breasts in half and fry with mushrooms in real butter. Pour in small amount of wine and brown. Place chicken in a glass baking pan sprayed with cooking spray.

Pour mushrooms and drippings over chicken. Mix soup and sour cream together and pour over chicken. Moisten stuffing with 1-1/2 cups boiling water. Spread over chicken.

Bake at 350 degrees for 45 minutes.

## CHICKEN PARMIGIANA

1 jar marinara sauce (get fresh in the refrigerated section of grocery store)
4 boneless skinless chicken breast halves
2/3 cup shredded mozzarella cheese
1 Tbsp. shredded Parmesan cheese
¼ cup Italian Style Bread Crumbs
2 Tbsp. olive oil
1 box Pillsbury Parmesan or Garlic and Herb breadsticks-prepared according to pkg. ½ to one box spaghetti cooked depending on number of chicken breasts served.

Heat oven to 350 degrees.

Pour marinara sauce evenly in bottom of ungreased 12" x 8" x 2 quart baking dish. Quick fry up the chicken breasts in extra virgin olive oil until slightly browned. Layer on top of marinara sauce. In small bowl, combine cheeses, bread crumbs and oil, mix well. Spread evenly over chicken. Bake at 350 degrees for 30-35 minutes until chicken is tender. Serve over plain cooked spaghetti and with breadsticks.
Yield: 4 servings

Note: Can increase to 6 pieces of chicken and use 13" x 9" baking dish. Boneless, skinless chicken thighs also work very well for those who prefer dark meat.
Recipe by Lynn Adgett

## CREAMED CHICKEN

2 Tbsp. butter
3 Tbsp. unbleached all-purpose flour
½ teaspoon sea salt
1 cup chicken broth (low sodium- no MSG)
1 cup low fat milk
2 cups cut up cooked chicken breast

Melt butter in frying pan. Remove from heat. Stir in flour until all blended. Add chicken broth and milk. Return to stove and stir on medium heat until thickened. Add chicken and serve on biscuits or toast.

## SKILLET CHICKEN POT PIE

1 can (10-3/4oz.) Healthy Request Cream of chicken soup
1-1/4 cups milk, divided
1 pkg. (10 oz.) frozen mixed vegetables or peas & carrots
2 cups diced cooked chicken
1 cup buttermilk biscuit baking mix
¼ teaspoon summer savory or parsley

Heat soup, 1 cup milk, vegetables and chicken in large skillet over medium heat until mixture comes to a boil. Combine, biscuit mix and summer savory or parsley in a small bowl. Stir in 2 to 3 tablespoons milk just until soft batter is formed. Drop batter by tablespoons onto chicken mixture to make six dumplings. Partially cover, simmer 12 minutes or until dumplings are cooked through, spooning liquid over dumplings once or twice during cooking. Garnish with additional summer savory if desired.

Yield: 6 servings

# CHICKEN POT PIE

1 can (10-3/4 oz.) Healthy Request Cream of Chicken soup
½ cup milk
1 package (12 oz. frozen) mixed vegetables (thawed) about 2-1/4 cups
1 cup cooked cubed chicken

Biscuit Topping
1-½ cups unbleached all-purpose flour
2 teaspoons Rumford baking powder
½ teaspoon baking soda
¾ teaspoon sea salt
½ cup buttermilk
¼ cup canola oil

Heat the oven to 400 degrees.

Stir the soup, ½ cup milk, vegetables and chicken in a 9" pie plate. Put flour, baking powder, baking soda and salt in medium sized mixing bowl. Pour buttermilk in 1 cup glass measuring cup. Add canola oil to the ¾ cup mark. Mix flour mixture well and add buttermilk and oil mixture all at once. Stir with fork to mix until it clings together.
Drop by tablespoons full onto pie and bake for 25 minutes or until bubbly.

# STIR FRIED CHICKEN & VEGETABLES

2 skinless, boneless chicken breasts
1 egg white
1 teaspoon cornstarch
1 teaspoon soy sauce (low sodium)
1 teaspoon sea salt
¼ teaspoon white pepper
1 can chicken broth (low sodium no MSG)
½ bag stir fry vegetables (broccoli, cauliflower and carrots)
6 Tbsp. canola oil

Mix egg white, soy sauce, cornstarch, salt and pepper in a medium sized bowl. Cut chicken into strips and add to egg white mixture. Chill in refrigerator for 30 minutes. Heat wok until a few drops of water bubble up. Add 3 tablespoons oil. Cook chicken stirring constantly until white. Empty into bowl and reserve. Add 3 tablespoons of oil to wok. Add stir fry vegetables. Sprinkle with garlic powder. Cook for a few minutes. Add chicken broth and bring to a boil and simmer for 10 minutes. Add reserved cooked chicken and cook for another 5 minutes. Add 2 tablespoons of cornstarch to thicken. Stir over hot rice.

Yield 3 servings.

## TURKEY TETRAZZINI

8 oz. linguine
3 Tbsp. butter
3 Tbsp. unbleached all-purpose flour
¼ teaspoon sea salt
1/8 teaspoon black pepper
1-1/2 cups low sodium chicken broth (No MSG)
½ cup heavy whipping cream
2 cups cubed cooked turkey
1 cup sliced mushrooms, cut up
1 small jar pimentos, (2 oz.)
1/8 cup chopped fresh parsley
¼ cup grated Parmesan cheese

Cook Pasta according to package direction. In a 10" nonstick frying pan, melt butter over medium heat. Stir in the flour, salt and pepper until smooth. Gradually add broth. Bring to a boil; cook and stir for 2 minutes or until thickened. Remove from heat and stir in cream. Drain linguine, add 1 cup sauce and toss to coat. Transfer to a greased 11" x 7" baking dish. Make a well in center about 6 inch by 4 inch. To remaining sauce, add turkey, mushrooms, pimentos and parsley. Pour in center of dish. Sprinkle with Parmesan cheese. Cover and bake at 350 degrees for 30 minutes. Uncover, and bake 20-30 minutes longer or until bubbly. Yield: 4 servings. Double recipe for 8 servings and use 1/3 cup Parmesan cheese and 1-4 oz. jar diced pimentos. Bake the same as above but use a greased 13" x9" baking pan.

# TURKEY HASH

¼ cup butter
¼ cup savory, crumbled
1 lb. ground turkey
½ cup chopped sweet onion
1-1/2 to 2 cups chopped and peeled baked potatoes
½ teaspoon sea salt
1/8 teaspoon pepper
1/8 teaspoon paprika

Brown butter, ground turkey and onions.  Cook until meat is done.  Stir in potatoes and spices.
Serve while hot.  Yield: 4 servings

# MICROWAVE RECIPES

## BAKED SWEET POTATO

1 small sweet potato, scrubbed
1 Tbsp. butter, room temperature
Sprinkle salt

Jab the sweet potato several times with tines of a fork. Wrap in paper towel and cook in microwave oven full power until soft, 4 to 5 minutes. Remove to a plate, cut open lengthwise, add the butter and salt, and enjoy while still hot. For variety you can add a sprinkling of cinnamon, nutmeg, or freshly ground black pepper.

## APPLE CRISP

6 to 8 medium to large cooking apples, peeled and sliced. Mackintosh or Empire work well.
½ cup butter, melted
¾-1 cup quick cooking oats
½ cup flour
1 teaspoon cinnamon

Spread apples in the bottom of a 11" x 7" glass baking dish. In a small glass bowl, melt butter In microwave (some models have a melt butter button) if not, use a low power setting (30%) For about 1 minute. Add remaining ingredients and mix with a fork until mixture is crumbly. Spread crumb mixture evenly over apples. Microwave for 10-12 minutes on high until apples are tender. Top with whipped cream, ice cream or custard sauce.

Recipe by Lynn Adgett

# CHOCOLATE PUDDING

¾ cup milk
3 Tbsp. semisweet chocolate chips
1 Tbsp. sugar
1 Tbsp. cornstarch
Dash of salt

In a 2 cup glass measuring cup, place milk and chips.
Microwave on High 1-1/2 minutes. Stir to melt. Combine
sugar, cornstarch and salt in bowl. Add to hot mixture. Stir
well. Microwave 1-1-1/2 minutes stirring after 30 seconds.
Spoon into serving dish. Yield: 1 serving

## Butterscotch Pudding

Follow recipe above except substitute butterscotch chips for
chocolate.

## SWEDISH MEATBALLS

1 large egg
¼ cup finely chopped sweet onion
¼ cup Italian bread crumbs
½ teaspoon sea salt
1/8 teaspoon pepper
2 teaspoons dried parsley or diced fresh parsley
¼ teaspoon ground nutmeg
1 lb. 93% ground beef
1 can (10-3/4 oz.) Healthy Request Cream of Mushroom Soup
¼ cup 2% milk
½ cup low fat sour cream
Hot cooked noodles

In a medium sized bowl, combine the egg, onion, bread crumbs, salt, pepper, parsley and nutmeg. Add the ground beef and mix well. Shape into 1-1/4 inch meatballs and place in an oblong microwave safe baking dish. Cover and microwave on high for 9-10 minutes or until meat is no longer pink. Combine the soup, milk and sour cream. Pour over meatballs. Cover and cook on high for 6 minutes. Sprinkle with additional parsley. Serve with noodles.

## BAKED APPLES

4 large Golden Delicious or Brae burn apples (about 2 lbs.)
¼ cup pitted prunes, chopped
2 Tbsp. raisins
2 Tbsp. brown sugar
2 teaspoons butter, softened
½ teaspoon ground cinnamon
1 teaspoon vanilla
Pinch of salt

Core apples, cutting a 1-1/4 inch diameter cylinder out of each apple's center, almost but not all the way through the bottom. Peel 1 inch ring of skin from around the top of each apple. Stand apples in 8" square baking pan or shallow 1-1/2 quart microwave safe casserole dish. In a small bowl, combine prunes, raisins, brown sugar, butter, cinnamon and salt and vanilla. Fill each cored apple with the fruit mixture. Microwave apples, covered on high until tender, about 8-12 minutes. Spoon any juices from dish over apples before serving.

## HAM SLICE

Place a 12 oz. to 1 lb. cooked slice of ham in a microwave safe dish. Cover with waxed paper. Microwave for 4 minutes.

SOUPS AND SALADS

## BROCCOLI CHEESE SOUP

2 cups low sodium chicken broth (No MSG)
1 package (16 oz.) frozen chopped broccoli or 16 ounces fresh broccoli chopped
1 medium sweet onion, chopped
¼ cup butter
3 Tbsp. unbleached all-purpose flour
1 cup milk (1 or 2 %)
8 oz. grated cheddar cheese

In a large saucepan, bring chicken broth to a boil.  Add broccoli.  Reduce heat; cover and simmer for 3-4 minutes or until tender-crisp.  Drain, reserving ¾ liquid.  In another large saucepan, sauté onion in butter until tender.  Whisk in flour until blended.  Add the milk and cheese.  Cook over medium-low heat until cheese is melted, stirring frequently.  Stir in broccoli and reserved cooking liquid.

Yield: 4 servings

## CREAM OF BROCCOLI SOUP

1-1/4 cups low-sodium chicken broth (No MSG)
3 cups broccoli flowerets
1 teaspoon olive oil
1 cup chopped sweet onion
½ teaspoon garlic powder
1-1/2 tablespoons cornstarch
2 cups evaporated skim milk or 1-3/4 cups soy milk
½ teaspoon sea salt
¼ teaspoon white pepper
3 Tbsp. fresh basil or 1-1/2 teaspoons dried basil
1/8 teaspoon ground nutmeg

Coarsely chop broccoli flowerets and boil in 1 cup chicken broth for about 5 minutes or until for tender. Set aside. Cool, and drain. In heavy skillet, sauté onion in olive oil until tender, about 8-10 minutes. Add chicken broth used to boil broccoli. Combine cornstarch with ¼ cup of chicken broth to form a smooth paste. Stir into skillet mixture over medium-low heat, whisking constantly until mixture thickens. Add cooked broccoli, milk, garlic powder, salt, pepper, basil and nutmeg. Bring to serving temperature, but do not boil.

Yield: 4 servings

## HARD TIMES BEAN SOUP

1 can (16 oz.) chopped tomatoes with juice
1 can (16 oz.) vegetarian baked beans in tomato sauce
1 cup water or reduced sodium chicken broth
¼ cup chopped sweet onion
½ teaspoon dried oregano
¼ teaspoon dried mustard or regular yellow mustard
½ cup shredded part-skim mozzarella cheese

Chop whole can tomatoes or use can of diced tomatoes. In medium saucepan, combine tomatoes, beans water, onion and seasoning. Cover and cook over medium heat for 15 minutes or until hot and onion is tender. Sprinkle each serving with 2 Tbsp. cheese. Makes 4 servings

## HAM AND CABBAGE SOUP

1 slice of fully cooked ham (approx. 12- oz. to 1 lb. pkg.) cut into cubes
4 medium potatoes, peeled and cubed
½ head of cabbage, cut into pieces
2 Tbsp. canola oil

In a large cooking pot on medium heat, cook ham in canola oil until browned. Add potatoes and cabbage and cover with water. Bring to a boil and simmer, covered, for ½ hr. or until vegetables are tender. Yield: 4 servings

Note: This recipe requires no salt because the ham is salty. You can season with pepper if desired.

# CREAMY ZUCCHINI SOUP

2 Tbsp. chopped sweet onion
3 Tbsp. butter
2 Tbsp. all-purpose unbleached flour
2 cups 2% or low fat milk
1-14 oz. can chicken broth (low sodium no MSG)
½ teaspoon sea salt
¼ teaspoon pepper
1 large zucchini or 2 small, shredded
1 cup (4 oz.) shredded cheddar cheese

In large saucepan, sauté onion in butter, until tender. Stir in flour until blended. Gradually stir in milk, 1 cup broth, salt and pepper. Bring to a boil; cook and stir for 2 minutes or until thickened. Add the zucchini. Simmer uncovered for 10 minutes until zucchini is tender. Stir in cheese and the rest of the chicken broth. When cheese is melted it is ready to serve.

Yield: 4 servings

## CREAMY ASPARAGUS SOUP

1 small sweet onion, finely chopped
½ cup butter, cubed
2 Tbsp. all-purpose unbleached flour
½ teaspoon garlic salt
¼ teaspoon pepper
2 cups low sodium chicken broth (No MSG)
2 cups milk
4 cups cut fresh asparagus (1 inch pieces)
1 cup mashed potatoes

In a large saucepan, sauté onion in butter until tender. Stir in the flour, garlic salt and pepper until blended. Gradually stir in the broth and milk. Add asparagus. Bring to a boil, cook and stir 2 minutes or until thickened. Reduce heat, simmer uncovered for 3-4 minutes or until asparagus is tender. Whisk in mashed potatoes until blended, heat through.

Yield: 5 servings

## CHILE CON CARNE

1-14.5 oz. can diced tomatoes
1 can Dark or Light Red Kidney beans, drained and rinsed
1 can Chili beans, undrained
½ cup diced sweet onion
1 Tbsp. extra virgin olive oil
1-lb. ground round beef
1 teaspoon garlic powder
1 cup low sodium chicken broth (No MSG)

Cook onions in olive oil until soft. Add ground round and cook until no longer pink. Pour can of tomatoes in a blender and puree. Add tomatoes, both kinds of beans, garlic powder and chicken broth to meat. Bring to a boil and simmer until ready to eat. Yield: 4 servings

## TURKEY NOODLE SOUP

1 cup thinly sliced celery
1 cup thinly sliced carrots
½ cup chopped sweet onion
1 teaspoon garlic powder or bottled minced garlic
¼ teaspoon sea salt
¼ teaspoon pepper
6 cups low sodium chicken broth (No MSG)
2 cups uncooked egg noodles
2 cups cooked, chopped turkey

Heat a soup pot over medium heat and spray with cooking spray. Add celery, carrots, onion and garlic. Cook until vegetables are soft. Add broth, salt, pepper, noodles and turkey. Cook until noodles are done. Yield: 4 servings

## LYNN'S HOMEMADE CHICKEN SOUP

Remnants of 1 Rotisserie Chicken
3 stalks celery washed and sliced
1 teaspoon minced garlic
3-4 stalks green onions, sliced
2 packages Ramen oriental flavor soup mix
1 package frozen spinach

In large stockpot, cover chicken parts with water and add celery, garlic and green onion. Bring to a boil. Pour chicken carcass into a strainer over a large bowl to save the liquid. Return the liquid to the pot. Break up ramen noodles and add flavor packets to the soup mixture. Heat until noodles are cooked. Cook the frozen spinach in microwave. Drain, salt and add half the spinach to the soup mixture. Store or eat the remaining spinach. Makes a large pot- 8-12 servings.
Note: If rotisserie chicken is not available use cooked, chopped chicken and boil with celery, garlic and onions.
Recipe by Lynn Adgett

## LEMON PINEAPPLE SALAD

1 (6 oz. package) lemon flavored gelatin
2 cups boiling water
1 (21 oz.) can lemon pie filling
1 (8 oz.) container frozen light whipped topping, thawed
1 (15 oz.) can crushed pineapple, undrained
2 teaspoons grated lemon rind

Stir together lemon flavored gelatin and 2 cups boiling water in a large bowl until dissolved. Chill 1 hr. or until consistency of unbeatable egg whites. Whisk in lemon pie filling and whipped topping until smooth. Fold in pineapple and lemon rind, spoon mixture into a lightly greased 2 quart mold or serving dish. (13" x 9" glass dish works fine.) Chill 8 hrs. or until firm.

## CHERRY JELLO SALAD

1 large package cherry flavored gelatin (6 oz.)
1 large can cherry pie filling
2 cups frozen light whipped topping, thawed

Prepare gelatin according to directions on package, add cherry pie filling, and blend well. Chill mixing occasionally. Before mixture is firm fold in whipped topping. Chill again until firm.

## LIME GELATIN SALAD

1 package (6 ounces) lime-flavored gelatin
1 cup boiling water
1 package (8 oz.) Neufchatel cream cheese, softened
½ teaspoon vanilla extract
1 can (15 oz.) mandarin oranges, drained
1 cup lemon-lime soda
½ cup chopped pecans
1 carton (8 oz.) light frozen whipped topping, thawed

Dissolve gelatin in water. In a mixing bowl, beat cream cheese until fluffy. Stir in gelatin mixture and beat until smooth. Stir in vanilla, oranges, pineapple, soda and pecans. Chill until mixture mounds slightly when dropped from a spoon. Fold in the whipped topping. Pour into a 13" x 9" dish. Refrigerate for 3 to 4 hrs. or until firm. Cut into squares. Yield: 16-20 servings

## PISTACHIO FRUIT SALAD

1 (4oz.) package pistachio flavor instant pudding and pie filling
1 (20 oz.) can crushed pineapple in juice (undrained)
1 cup miniature marshmallows
½ cup chopped pecans
1-1/2 cups light whipped topping, thawed

Mix dry pudding mix, pineapple, marshmallows, and pecans in large bowl until well blended. Gently stir in whipped topping; cover. Refrigerate 1 hour or until ready to serve.

## COTTAGE CHEESE AND GELATIN SALAD

1 large can (20 oz.) crushed pineapple
1 (3 oz.) box gelatin (any flavor)
1-8 oz. carton frozen light whipped topping, thawed
1 lb. carton small curd cottage cheese

Heat pineapple in saucepan, sprinkle gelatin in pineapple while hot and mix well. Put in refrigerator until it begins to set. Stir in cottage cheese and whipped topping. Mix well and let set.

## ORANGE GELATIN SALAD

1 (3oz.) box orange gelatin
1 (1 lb.) carton of small curd cottage cheese
1 (8-1/4 oz.) can crushed pineapple, drained
1 (8oz.) carton frozen light whipped topping, thawed

Sprinkle gelatin over cottage cheese. Mix well. Add drained pineapple and mix well. Fold in whipped topping. Refrigerate or can be eaten as soon as it is made.
Yield: 4 servings

## CRANBERRY SALAD

1 can sweetened condensed milk
¼ cup freshly squeezed lemon juice
2 cups miniature marshmallows
1 can (16 oz.) whole berry cranberry sauce
1 can (20 oz.) crushed pineapple, drained
½ cup chopped pecans or walnuts
1-8oz. carton of light whipped topping, thawed

In a large bowl, whisk together sweetened condensed milk
and lemon juice. Stir in marshmallows, cranberry sauce,
crushed pineapple and chopped pecans.  Fold in whipped
topping and mix well.  Spread in 13 x 9 glass pan. Freeze until
firm about 4 hours or overnight.  Cut into squares and serve.
Yield 18 servings.


## ASIAN STEAK SALAD

1 bag fresh spinach
2 (6 oz.) sirloin steaks, grilled with Monterey steak spice
1 lb. baby Portabella mushrooms sautéed in butter, then
refrigerated until cold
2 medium tomatoes
Fresh bacon bits
1 small package (6 oz.) walnuts

Mix cooled spinach with steak which has been sliced into
strips.  Cut mushrooms and tomatoes and add.  Add bacon
bits and walnuts to taste.  Serve with Asian dressing.

## CUCUMBER TOMATO SALAD

1 large cucumber washed, peeled and sliced
1 medium sized tomato cut up small
¼ cup sweet onion cut up
1 Tbsp. cider vinegar
1 Tbsp. canola oil
Salt & pepper to taste
Place cucumber, tomato and onion in a medium sized bowl.
Add vinegar, salt & pepper. Mix well and then add oil and
mix thoroughly.  Yield: 2 servings
Variation:  Add fresh mozzarella balls, halved.

## COLESLAW

½ of a large head of cabbage, grated
1 small carrot, grated
1 Tbsp. grated sweet onion
½ cup light mayonnaise
2 Tbsp. sugar or 1 small packet of Stevia
2 Tbsp. milk
Salt to taste

Combine cabbage, carrots and sweet onion in medium bowl.
Combine remaining ingredients, add salt to taste.  Cover and
chill until ready to serve.  Makes 4 servings

## BLACK BEAN SALAD

2 cans (15 oz. each) black beans, rinsed and drained
1 pint cherry tomatoes, quartered
1 medium sweet yellow or green pepper, julienned
½ cup chopped sweet onion
3 Tbsp. minced fresh parsley

Dressing:
2 Tbsp. extra virgin olive oil
3 Tbsp. lemon juice
½ teaspoon garlic powder or bottled minced garlic
½ teaspoon cumin
½ teaspoon sea salt
¼ teaspoon pepper

In a large salad bowl, combine the beans, tomatoes, pepper, onions and parsley.

Combine dressing ingredients in a small bowl and drizzle over vegetables and toss to coat. Chill until serving.
Yield: 8 servings

## SHRIMP PASTA SALAD

4 cups cooked small pasta shells
1 lb. cooked large shrimp, peeled, deveined, and cut into thirds
1 cup frozen peas
½ cup chopped green onions
¼ cup minced fresh parsley
1 cup (8 oz.) plain yogurt
1 cup light mayonnaise
¼ cup fresh lemon juice
2 Tbsp. snipped fresh dill
½ teaspoon sea salt
¼ teaspoon white pepper

In a bowl, combine the pasta, shrimp, peas, onions and parsley.  In a small bowl, combine the yogurt, mayonnaise, lemon juice, dill, salt and pepper.  Pour over pasta mixture and toss gently. Cover and refrigerate for at least 2 hours before serving.  Yield: 10 servings

## SPINACH SALAD

½ lb. fresh spinach leaves
2 hard cooked eggs
½ cup finely diced Sharp Cheddar cheese
¼ cup minced sweet onion
1 teaspoon cider vinegar
¾ cup light mayonnaise
¼ teaspoon Tabasco sauce
½ teaspoon sea salt

Wash spinach thoroughly, drain and dry. Finely chop, spinach and eggs. Add salt, Tabasco and vinegar to mayonnaise. Combine all ingredients and serve.

## GREEN PEA AND BEET SALAD

1 can (15 oz.) diced beets, drained and rinsed.
3 large hard cooked eggs, peeled and chopped
½ cup sweet onion, diced
1 medium rib celery, diced
1 cup frozen peas, thawed
½ Tbsp. sugar
3/8 cup mayonnaise

Chill the beets in the refrigerator. Place chopped eggs in a medium bowl. Mix in the onion and celery; set aside. Put the beets in a large bowl and gently stir in the peas. Add the egg mixture, mayonnaise and sugar; mix well. Spread individual lettuce on plates and place a scoop of salad on each.
Note: Use ½ lb. of fresh beets, boiled, trimmed, peeled and diced in place of the canned beets. Yield: 3 servings

## MACARONI SALAD

2 cups cooked elbow macaroni
1 large tomato, chopped
1 cup frozen peas, thawed
½ cup shredded cheddar cheese
½ cup chopped celery
1 hard cooked egg, chopped
2 green onions chopped or ¼ cup sweet onion chopped

Dressing:
¾ cup light mayonnaise
1 cup plain yogurt
2 Tbsp. sugar
1 Tbsp. mustard

In a large bowl, combine the macaroni, tomato, peas, cheese, celery, egg and onions. In a small bowl, combine the dressing ingredients. Pour over macaroni mixture and toss to coat. Refrigerate until serving. Yield: 10 servings

## FRESH FRUIT DINNER SALAD

2 cups rotisserie chicken, cut up
6 large strawberries, cut up
1/3 cup blueberries
¼ cup sliced almonds
1/8 cup chopped sweet onion
2 cups tender Ruby Red lettuce
¼ cup diced Landana Curry Coconut cheese from Holland
(available at Sam's Club)

Layer lettuce, fruit, chicken, onion, and cheese. Sprinkle with almonds. Serve with Greek Vinaigrette dressing or dressing of your choice. Yield: 2 servings
Recipe by Lynn Adgett

## WINTER FRUIT PASTA SALAD

1 cup uncooked small pasta shells (4oz.)
1 medium apple, chopped (1-1/4 cups)
1 medium pear, chopped (1-1/4 cups)
4 medium green onions, chopped (1/4 cup)
¼ cup chopped or broken pecans
¼ cup dried cranberries
1/3 cup mayonnaise or salad dressing
3 Tbsp. orange marmalade
½ teaspoon dried marjoram
¼ teaspoon salt

1. Cook and drain pasta as directed on package. Rinse with cold water, drain.
2. Mix pasta, apple, pear, onion, pecans and cranberries in large glass or plastic bowl.
3. Cover and refrigerate at least 30 minutes until chilled.
    Yield: 8 servings. Recipe by Lynn Adgett

## RASPBERRY CHICKEN SALAD

5 cups salad greens
2 cups cut-up rotisserie chicken
1 cup fresh raspberries cleaned and drained
½ cup diced celery
¼ cup diced sweet onion

Dressing
1 small carton of plain yogurt
½ cup fresh raspberries
1 Tbsp. red wine vinegar
2 teaspoons sugar or 2 packets of Stevia

Place all ingredients in blender. Cover and blend on high speed until smooth. Toss salad greens, chicken, raspberries, celery and onion. Serve with dressing.

VEGETABLES

## CAULIFLOWER AU GRATIN

1 cup chicken broth (low sodium, no MSG)
1 large head of cauliflower broken into florets or 20 oz. bag
frozen cauliflower
¼ cup butter cubed
¼ cup seasoned bread crumbs
½ cup shredded Parmesan cheese

In a large saucepan bring broth to a boil. Add cauliflower.
Reduce heat to medium, cover and cook for 15-18 minutes or
until tender. Meanwhile in a small skillet, melt butter. Add
bread crumbs, cook and stir for 3-5 minutes or until toasted
and browned. Remove from the heat. Drain cauliflower, add
cheese and mix thoroughly. Place in a serving bowl and top
with crumbs. Note: If using frozen cauliflower, allow package
to thaw slightly on counter before cooking.

## BAKED SUMMER SQUASH

2 summer squash, washed and cut across in slices
½ cup sweet onion, sliced
2 Tbsp. butter
2 Tbsp. canola oil
Sea salt and pepper

Melt butter in an 11″ x 7″ baking dish on top of stove on low
or in the microwave. Layer sliced squash in dish. Cover with
sliced onions. Season with salt and pepper and bake in a 400
degree oven for 25 minutes or until squash is tender.

## LOIS'S STEWED TOMATOES

1 (14.5 oz.) can diced tomatoes
1 Tbsp. sugar or small packet of Stevia
1 Tbsp. cornstarch
1 teaspoon butter

Pour tomatoes into small cooking pot.  Add sugar or stevia.
Bring to a boil and add cornstarch that has been mixed with a
small amount of water.  Stir constantly until tomatoes thicken,
add butter.  You can use diced canned tomatoes that have
been seasoned with garlic and oregano.

Very good served over homemade Macaroni & Cheese.

# BEST SCALLOPED POTATOES

Butter for greasing pan
2 peeled and smashed garlic cloves or 2 Tbsp. minced garlic
2 cups 2 % milk
Fresh nutmeg, grated to taste, or ground nutmeg
Kosher salt
Freshly ground black pepper
2 lbs. Yukon Gold potatoes
1 cup grated Havarti Swiss cheese
1 cup thick grated Parmesan cheese

Preheat oven to 425 degrees. Butter 9" x 13" baking dish or casserole. Place garlic, milk, nutmeg, salt and pepper in a pot, stir, and then heat until simmering around the edges. Meanwhile, rinse the potatoes, then slice finely using a food processor. If you don't have a food processor, then slice with a sharp knife very carefully into thin rounds. Do not rinse potatoes after they have been sliced. Add potatoes to milk mixture, increase heat to bring to a boil, then reduce heat to simmer for 15 minutes or until potatoes are tender. Dump the potatoes and milk sauce into the buttered baking dish and taste the sauce. Add more salt, pepper or nutmeg to your taste, if desired. Sprinkle with the cheese. Cook about 45 minutes, or until cheese is browned and bubbling and potatoes are tender. Let stand for 15 minutes before serving
Recipe by Lynn Adgett

## TENDER ROASTED POTATOES

3 lbs. small red potatoes, scrubbed and diced
2 Tbsp. canola oil
1/3 cup prepared horseradish sauce
¼ cup whole grain mustard
2 Tbsp. butter, melted.

In a large bowl, toss potatoes with oil.  Place potatoes on greased baking sheet.  Bake at 400 degrees for 30 minutes.  Meanwhile in a small bowl, combine the horseradish sauce, mustard and butter.  Spoon over potatoes and toss to coat.  Bake 5-7 minutes longer or until tender.
Yield: 10 servings
Recipe by Lynn Adgett

## GREEN BEANS WITH FRENCH ONIONS

1 lb. fresh green beans, washed and broken into pieces
1 cup French fried onions
1 Tbsp. butter

Cook green beans in saucepan with water or in a steamer until tender.  Drain and add French onions and butter.  Stir until butter is completely melted.  Yield: 4 servings

## OVEN HASH BROWNS

1 pkg. "Simply potatoes" Hash Browns
½ cup finely chopped sweet onion
1 teaspoon sea salt
¼ teaspoon pepper
2 Tbsp. butter melted
2 Tbsp. canola oil

Heat oven to 400 degrees. Squeeze potatoes between paper
towels to remove moisture. Toss potatoes with onion, salt and
pepper in large bowl. Pour butter and oil into 9" x 13" baking
dish; add potato mixture. Bake 20 to 25 minutes, turning once,
until golden brown. Yield: 6 servings

## MASHED POTATOES & TURNIPS

1 large potato, peeled and cut up small
1 turnip, peeled and cut up small
3 Tbsp. sweet onion
3 Tbsp. butter
Hot milk

Place potato and turnip in a cooking pot and cover with water.
Sprinkle with sea salt. Bring to a boil and boil for 25 minutes.
Meanwhile cook 3 Tbsp. sweet onion in 1 Tbsp. butter until
brown. When potatoes are tender, drain and mash with
remaining 2 Tbsp. butter. Add enough hot milk to make
smooth. Add onions. Yield: 2 servings

## SEA SALT SWEET POTATOES

2 lbs. (about 3 medium) Sweet Potatoes or yams peeled and cut into 1' pieces
½ tsp. coarse sea salt
2 Tbsp. vegetable, canola or olive oil
¼ teaspoon black pepper
¼ cup Maple Syrup
¼ cup pecan pieces

Preheat oven to 425 degrees and coat 9" x 13" baking dish with cooking spray. Mix all ingredients together in a separate bowl, except for pecans. Arrange mixture in baking pan. Bake for 25-30 minutes, stirring half-way through. Remove from oven and sprinkle with pecan pieces. Finish with a pinch of sea salt and serve. Yield: 4-6 servings

Note: To prepare faster, cook diced sweet potatoes in ½ cup water in microwave for 10 minutes, then finish by baking. Also these can tend to burn easily with the maple syrup, check and toss frequently.

Recipe by Lynn Adgett

## CANDIED YAMS

5 small yams
1/3 cup firmly packed light brown sugar
¼ teaspoon ground cinnamon
¼ teaspoon sea salt
2 Tbsp. honey
4 Tbsp. fresh orange juice

Boil yams for 15 minutes. Drain and cool. Peel with a potato peeler and slice each yam in half. Place in a - 9" x 13" baking dish that has been sprayed with cooking spray. Mix brown sugar, honey, orange juice, cinnamon and salt in a small bowl. Drizzle over sweet potatoes. Bake at 350 degrees, covered for 45 minutes and uncovered for 15 minutes. Yield: 5 servings

## SOUTHERN CORN PUDDING

3 eggs well beaten
1-1/2 cups 2% milk
3 Tbsp. unbleached all-purpose flour
3 Tbsp. sugar
1 teaspoon sea salt
1 (14-1/2 to 15-1/2 oz.) can cream style corn
3 Tbsp. butter

Blend flour, sugar and salt. Add to beaten eggs and whip smooth. Add milk, blend, then add corn. Pour into greased 2-1/2 quart casserole, dot with butter broken into small pieces. Bake at 375 degrees for 45 minutes to 1 hour. Yield: 6 servings

# MISCELLANEOUS

## LOIS'S HOT FUDGE SAUCE

2 squares unsweetened chocolate
½ stick butter (1/4 cup)
½ cup sugar
½ cup light corn syrup
½ can fat free evaporated milk (6 oz.)
1 teaspoon vanilla

Melt chocolate and butter in saucepan over low heat. Add sugar, corn syrup and evaporated milk. Cook until it comes to a boil. Boil for 1 minute. Remove from stove and add vanilla. Pour into a pint size glass jar. Pour over ice cream.
Yield: 1 pint

## APPLE CRUNCH TOPPING

2 medium apples, cored and sliced
2 Tbsp. melted butter
1/3 cup walnuts
¼ cup maple syrup
2 Tbsp. cinnamon sugar

In a skillet over medium heat cook apples in butter for 3 minutes or until just beginning to soften. Stir in walnuts, maple syrup and cinnamon sugar. Toss mixture to coat. Reduce heat to low and cook 2 minutes more or until apples are completely softened. Serve over vanilla ice cream or vanilla frozen yogurt.

## PEACH BUTTER

3 cups sliced fresh peaches (about 4 large)
¼ cup orange juice
¾ cup sugar
2 Tbsp. honey
½ teaspoon grated orange rind
1/8 teaspoon ground allspice

Combine peaches and orange juice in a saucepan, bring to a boil. Cover, reduce heat and simmer 8 minutes or until tender, stirring occasionally. Process mixture in a blender or food processor until smooth, stopping to scrape down sides. Return peach mixture to saucepan; add sugar and remaining ingredients. Bring to a boil; reduce heat, and simmer, uncovered, 25 minutes or until thickened, stirring occasionally. Spoon into jars, cover and store in refrigerator.

Yield: 1-1/2 cups

## GRILLED CORN ON THE COB

4 ears of corn (husks and silk removed)
2 Tbsp. soft butter
½ teaspoon garlic powder
Heavy Duty aluminum foil

Place cleaned corn in cold water for 15 minutes. Remove and dry. Place each ear on a square of aluminum foil (enough to wrap well.) Mix butter and garlic powder in a small bowl. Brush on each ear of corn covering it entirely. Wrap each individual corn and fold under ends. Grill for 10 minutes on one side and then turn over and grill for 10 minutes on the other side. Delicious
Note: For 8 ears of corn, double the recipe.

## LOIS'S PICKLED BEETS

1-14.5 oz. can of sliced beets
½ cup cider vinegar
½ cup sugar
½ teaspoon salt
½ cup beet juice

Reserve beet juice from can and empty beets into a medium sized cooking pot. Add ½ cup beet juice, vinegar, sugar and salt. Bring to a boil and simmer for 20 minutes.

## BAKED BEAN PATTIES (Meatless Meal)

1- (14.5 oz. can baked beans preferably vegetarian)
2- ½ cup Italian bread crumbs
3- ½ cup grated carrot
4- 1/3 cup finely chopped onion.

Mix all ingredients well (Add water to moisten, if necessary.) Using 1/3 cup each, shape mixture into 6 patties; coat with additional fine bread crumbs. Cook patties in 2 Tbsp. butter till browned on both sides, 5 minutes per side.

## HELPFUL HINTS

Equivalents- Citrus Fruit
1 lemon = 3 Tbsp. juice &
              2 teaspoons peel
1 lime =    2 Tbsp. juice &
              1 teaspoon peel
1 orange = 1/3 cup to ½ cup juice
              & 2 Tbsp. peel

Cleaning Vegetables & Fruits
Use 1 part cider vinegar to 1 part cold water and put in Plastic
Spray bottle. If they are highly waxed, use dishwashing soap
detergent such as Palmolive with Aloe Vera and scrub them
until all wax is removed. Rinse with water. Then use the
vinegar water. Rinse and dry.

Homemade Baking Powder
Sift together:
2 Tbsp. cream of tartar
1 Tbsp. cornstarch
1 Tbsp. baking soda
Combine and store in an airtight container. One teaspoon of
this baking power is equal to one teaspoon of the store bought
kind.

## HANDY SUBSTITUTIONS

Buttermilk = 1 cup milk plus 1 Tbsp. white or cider vinegar
1 cup self-rising flour = 1 cup unbleached all-purpose flour
plus 1 teaspoon baking powder, plus ½ teaspoon sea salt

1 cup cake flour = 1 cup sifted unbleached all-purpose flour
minus 2 Tbsp. Add 2 Tbsp. cornstarch.

1 cup powdered sugar = 1 cup sugar plus 1 Tbsp. cornstarch.
Process this in a food processor or blender.

1 cup light corn syrup = 1 cup sugar plus ¼ cup water

1 Tbsp. cornstarch = 2 Tbsp. unbleached all-purpose flour

1 (1 oz.) chocolate square = 3 Tbsp. cocoa plus 1 Tbsp. butter

½ cup balsamic vinegar = ½ cup red wine vinegar

1 medium onion chopped = 1 Tbsp. onion powder

1 garlic clove = 1/8 teaspoon garlic powder

1 Tbsp. chopped fresh herbs = 1 teaspoon dried herbs or ¼
teaspoon powdered herbs

1 teaspoon ground allspice = ½ teaspoon ground cinnamon
plus ½ teaspoon ground cloves

67673812R00075

Made in the USA
Charleston, SC
17 February 2017